Elizabeth I's Last Favourite

Robert Devereux, 2nd Earl of Essex

Elizabeth I's Last Favourite

Robert Devereux, 2nd Earl of Essex

Sarah-Beth Watkins

Winchester, UK
Washington, USA

JOHN HUNT PUBLISHING

First published by Chronos Books, 2021
Chronos Books is an imprint of John Hunt Publishing Ltd., No. 3 East St., Alresford,
Hampshire SO24 9EE, UK
office@jhpbooks.com
www.johnhuntpublishing.com
www.chronosbooks.com

For distributor details and how to order please visit the 'Ordering' section on our website.

ISBN: 978 1 78904 595 6
978 1 78904 596 3 (ebook)
Library of Congress Control Number: 2020933109

A CIP catalogue record for this book is available from the British Library.

Design: Stuart Davies

UK: Printed and bound by CPI Group (UK) Ltd, Croydon, CR0 4YY
Printed in North America by CPI GPS partners

We operate a distinctive and ethical publishing philosophy in
all areas of our business, from our global network of authors to
production and worldwide distribution.

Contents

Chapter One: The Early Years 1565–1585   1

Chapter Two: Essex's First Command 1586–1587   18

Chapter Three: The Spanish Threat 1588–1590   31

Chapter Four: The French Campaign 1591–1592   45

Chapter Five: The Lopez Plot 1593–1594   56

Chapter Six: A Voyage to Cadiz 1595–1596   72

Chapter Seven: To the Azores 1597–1598   89

Chapter Eight: Essex's Final Command 1599   105

Chapter Nine: The Essex Rebellion 1600–1601   118

Chapter Ten: The Earl's Descendants   136

Appendix One: His Last Poem   143

References   156

Select Bibliography   164

Also by Sarah-Beth Watkins

Lady Katherine Knollys: The Unacknowledged Daughter of King Henry VIII

The Tudor Brandons: Mary and Charles – Henry VIII's Nearest & Dearest

Margaret Tudor, Queen of Scots: The Life of King Henry VIII's Sister

Anne of Cleves: Henry VIII's Unwanted Wife

Catherine of Braganza: Charles II's Restoration Queen

The Tragic Daughters of Charles I

Sir Francis Bryan: Henry VIII's Most Notorious Ambassador
Ireland's Suffragettes

Books for Writers:
Telling Life's Tales
Life Coaching for Writers
The Lifestyle Writer
The Writer's Internet

To Plead My Faith...
To plead my faith where faith had no reward,
To move remorse where favour is not bourne,
To heap complaints where she doth not regard, —
Were fruitless, bootless, vain, and yield but scorn.

I lovéd her whom all the world admired,
I was refused of her that can love none;
And my vain hopes, which far too high aspired,
Is dead, and buried, and for ever gone.

Forget my name, since you have scorned my love,
And woman-like do not too late lament;
Since for your sake I do all mischief prove,
I none accuse nor nothing do repent.

I was as fond as ever she was fair,
Yet loved I not more than I now despair.
Robert Devereux, 2ⁿᵈ Earl of Essex

Robert Devereux, 2nd Earl of Essex and Queen Elizabeth I's last favourite, climbed the scaffold and delivered his well thought out speech. He had had days to rehearse it as he paced his room in the Tower of London. How has it come to this? he wondered. All he had wanted was glory and fame, to serve his queen and have her love him. Love him like she had loved his stepfather.

As he uttered the words 'I desire all the world to forgive me, even as I do freely and from my heart forgive all the world...' he knew he had never accomplished that. If Elizabeth had truly loved him she would have saved him. She would have listened to him, she would have forgiven him.

Once she had twirled his long dark hair in her fingers and caressed his face whispering sweet endearments. He had not shied away from her bad breath or wizened fingers. She was his queen, his sovereign and the maker of his fortunes. But then had come the arguments, the anger, the violence and the drawn sword.

He had never wanted to go to Ireland but she had made him. All he had wanted when he rode at breakneck speed across England was to return to her. Bursting into her rooms, he had seen an old woman in her bed clothes, frail and vulnerable, and he knew now that she had seen the possibility of her own death at his hand.

He had tried so hard to talk to her but those other men that rallied around her wouldn't let him get close any more. He had tried to force his way to her. If only he had been able to reach her, all would have been forgiven. Or that is what he had thought at the time. Now he wasn't so sure and as the executioner's axe descended he thought no more.

Chapter One

The Early Years

1565–1585

Robert Devereux who would become the 2nd Earl of Essex and Queen Elizabeth I's last favourite was born on 10th November 1565 in the manor house at Netherwood near Bromyard, in Herefordshire. His life was to be short and turbulent. He would rise in the queen's favour, triumphing over all his enemies, but his relationship with Elizabeth would always be fractious. He sought glory and engaged in military action in the Netherlands, France, Cadiz, the Azores and Ireland. After developing an intelligence network to rival the Cecils, he was a key player in the political life of the Elizabethan court. But as he rose to the heights of his ambition, he would also fall in devastating circumstances all of his own making.

Robert was the eldest son born to Walter Devereux, 1st Earl of Essex and mother Lettice Knollys in 1565.[1] When Robert's parents were married five years before, his father Walter was high in the queen's favour and his mother Lettice was one of her ladies-in-waiting. She was the daughter of Francis and Katherine Knollys who became important figures during Elizabeth's reign; Francis as treasurer of the royal household and privy councillor and Katherine as chief lady of the bedchamber. Grandmother Katherine was the daughter of Mary Boleyn then married to William Carey but also Henry VIII's mistress. It is quite possible that Katherine was actually the king's daughter and that Robert therefore had inherited royal blood on his maternal side.[2]

Robert may have been named after Robert of Evreux, the first of his paternal family to arrive in England with William the Conqueror and establish the Devereux line. Robert Dudley, Earl of Leicester and Elizabeth I's favourite stood as his godfather so he may also have been named after the famous courtier. Dudley certainly stood for other children at the time including the sons of Sir Nicholas Throckmorton, Lord Paget and Sir Philip Sidney and the earl would later play a large role in Robert's life.

Robert's father, Walter Devereux, was created 2nd Viscount Hereford and 10th Baron Ferrers of Chartley, Bourchier and Lovaine after his grandfather's death in 1558. Chartley, a moated house with extensive gardens in Stowe-by-Chartley, Staffordshire, was close to the ruins of a castle abandoned as a residence in 1485 when a new house was built. Robert would grow up in the new manor house with his sisters Penelope and Dorothy born before him in 1563 and 1564 and a younger brother Walter born in 1569.

In the same year Devereux's last son was born, Mary Queen of Scots was housed at Tutbury not far from their family home at Chartley. Walter was ordered to organise a body of men and horses to prevent any rescue attempts. On the queen's command he then travelled north with his men to suppress the rising of the northern earls – an attempt by Catholic nobles to overthrow Elizabeth I and replace her with her cousin Mary. For his loyalty and actions, Walter Devereux was made a Knight of the Garter closely followed by his creation as the Earl of Essex in 1572. The queen was well pleased with him but his relationship with her favourite, the Earl of Leicester, was increasingly troubled. Walter was 'so great a favorite that Leicester [Dudley] and others [were] jealous of his increasing influence'.[3]

Elizabeth granted permission for Walter to 'embark in a scheme for subduing part of Ulster, expelling the Scotch and islesman, and colonizing it with English[men]'.[4] It was said by some that Leicester wanted him out of the way as he was having an affair with young Robert's mother, Lettice. Walter was 'put upon this adventure by Leicester who loved the Earl's nearest relation [Lettice] better than he loved the Earl himself'. Rumours suggested the earl wanted to 'plunge him into dangers under pretense of procuring him honor'.[5]

Devereux left for Ireland in the autumn of 1573 and would stay there until November 1575. It gave the rumour mill a chance to continue spreading aspersions about the queen's favourite and Lady Essex. The queen had been aware of a flirtation between them as far back as 1565, the year Robert was born, which led to stories that Leicester was in fact Robert's father. Dudley however still held out hope that one day Elizabeth would agree to marry him. She had made him jealous by flirting with Thomas Heneage, a Gentleman of the Privy Chamber. It seems that Leicester wanted to 'devise some means to find out whether the Queen was really as much attached to him as she appeared to be'.[6] Sir Nicholas Throckmorton suggested he 'fall in love himself with one of the ladies in the palace and watch how the Queen took it' so he paid court to Lettice 'one of the best looking ladies' there.[7] Elizabeth's reaction could have been predicted. Initially she was furious but then forgave him. A pattern that would be played out repeatedly in later years with both Leicester and Robert.

According to the Spanish Ambassador Diego Guzmán de Silva,

> *The Queen was in a great temper and upbraided him with what had taken place with Heneage and his flirting with the Viscountess in very bitter words. He went down to his apartments and stayed there for three or four days until the Queen sent for him, the earl of Sussex and Cecil having tried to smooth the business over, although they are no friends of Lord Robert in their hearts. The result of the tiff was that both the Queen and Robert shed tears, and he has returned to his former favour.*[8]

The queen's summer progress of 1575 took her to the Earl of Leicester's home, Kenilworth Castle, but she seemed oblivious to what was apparently a renewal of Robert and Lettice's relationship. Not so others. One Edward Arden, former High Sheriff of Warwickshire, refused to wear Dudley's livery calling the earl a 'whore-master'[9] and told everyone of frequent assignations between the queen's favourite and Lady Essex. Elizabeth continued on to Chartley so there was no hint of any animosity towards Lettice at this point. She may even have seen young Robert here with his siblings, Penelope, Dorothy and Walter.

When Walter Devereux returned from Ireland later in the year the new Spanish ambassador Antonio de Guaras reported that:

> As the thing is publicly talked of in the streets, there can be no harm in my writing openly about the great enmity between the Earl of Leicester and the Earl of Essex, in consequence, it is said, of the fact that while Essex was in Ireland his wife had two children by Leicester...Great discord is expected in consequence.[10]

In *Leicester's Commonwealth* published later in 1584 it stated when Walter

> was coming home from Ireland with intent to revenge himself upon my Lord of Leicester for begetting his wife with child in his absence (the child was a daughter and brought up by the Lady Shandoies, W. Knooles' his wife), my Lord of Leicester hearing thereof, wanted not a friend or two to accompany the deputy, as among other, a couple of the Earl's own servants, Crompton (if I miss not his name), yeoman of his bottles, and Lloyd, his secretary, entertained afterward by my Lord of Leicester.[11]

There is no evidence of any children born to Lettice during that time. Neither was there any major altercation between Devereux and Dudley on Walter's return so it may have all just been rumour and suspicion at this point.

The Earl of Leicester may well have been enamoured of

Lady Essex but he had been having an affair with Lady Douglas Sheffield and their son was born in 1574. Lady Sheffield swore they had been married but with no proof and Dudley's denial, their son would be illegitimate. By 1576 however his father was overseeing his care and taking responsibility for his education. It is uncertain when the earl's affair with Lady Sheffield ended and it overlaps with rumours of his supposed liaison with Lady Essex whilst she was still married. Leicester was the queen's favourite and not without enemies who would continually spread malicious stories in a bid to bring him down.

The queen was yet to show any animosity to Lettice and she was impressed with her husband Walter's service in Ireland, although a horrendous massacre at Rathlin Island was yet to occur, telling him he had brought 'Ulster into obedience and quiet'.[12] He was made Earl Marshal and Elizabeth wrote to him 'the search of your honour, with the danger of your breath, hath not been bestowed on so ungrateful a Prince that will not both consider the one and reward the other'.[13]

Walter travelled back to Ireland in July 1576 but the rumours about his wife and the queen's favourite would persist for years especially given later circumstances. At the end of August Walter became ill after dining with 'grief in his belly'. A servant was also taken ill and Walter wrote to Richard Broughton telling him it 'maketh me suspect of some evil received in my drink'.[14]

By September Walter was severely ill with what was probably dysentery. He sent a letter to the queen from his sickbed

My humble suit must yet extend itself further into many branches, for the behoof of my poor children, that since God doth now make them fatherless, yet it would please your Majesty to be as a mother unto them, at least by your gracious countenance and care of their education and matches. Mine eldest son, upon whom the continuation of my house remaineth, shall lead a life far unworthy his calling and most obscurely, if it be not holpen by your Majesty's bounty and favour; for the smallness of his living, the greatness of my debt, and the dowries that go out of my land, make the remainder little or nothing towards the reputation of an Earl's estate.[15]

What is particularly interesting is that he talks of Robert specifically. If he had any doubts about his parentage, would he have singled him out thus? He wrote one more letter to Lord Burghley asking that he look after his son and 'bind him with perpetual friendship' in the hope that Robert would 'grow up to reverence your Lord for wisdom and gravity, and lay up your counsels and advice in the treasury of his heart'.[16] Sir Henry Wotton would later claim that the earl had a 'cold conceit' for his son but again this would be written later amongst rumours of Leicester and Lettice's relationship and the proof of his will and last letters refute this.

Walter died on 22 September. It was reported that on his deathbed he said 'Lord forgive me and forgive all the world, Lord, from the bottom of my heart, from the bottom of my heart even all the injuries and wrongs that any have done unto me! Lord forgive them, and I forgive them from the bottom of my heart'.[17] Some have taken this to mean he forgave his wife for her indiscretion. If he wrote to Lettice from Ireland his letter did not survive.

Sir Edward Waterhouse, Walter's secretary, wrote to Sir Henry Sidney 'I do not think that there is at this day so strong a man in England of friends, as the little Earl of Essex, nor any man more lamented than his father'.[18]

Whether any of the rumours of his parentage affected Robert during his childhood is hard to say. We will never know whether Robert was truly Walter's son. The facts certainly point to his mother having an affair with Leicester but yet more evidence shows that Walter was more likely Robert's father. However as he grew older, the queen would definitely see something in him that spoke to her of her one true love, the Earl of Leicester.

The rumours didn't stop with Devereux's death. It was said that Dudley had had the earl poisoned so that he could be with the man's wife. It did not help that Walter himself had at first suspected his drink may have been poisoned. *Leicester's Commonwealth* which certainly had nothing good to say about the Lady Essex and the queen's favourite suggested 'And so he died in the way, of an extreme flux, caused by an Italian recipe, as all his friends are well assured, the maker whereof was a surgeon (as is believed) that then was newly come to my Lord from Italy'.[19] At the time the stories were persuasive enough for Sir Henry Sidney to conduct a post-mortem examination. Not only was the finger pointed at Leicester but at Lettice as well although the enquiry showed no trace of poison.

The young Robert appears to have been ill and unable to attend his father's funeral in Carmarthen, Walter's birthplace. It had been delayed due to the post-mortem and he wrote to Lord Burghley, his new guardian, in November 1576 to pardon him for his 'weak body'.[20] His correspondence was sent on to the Lord Treasurer by Sir Edward Waterhouse whose accompanying letter remarked how Robert could 'express his mind in Latin and French, as well as in English, very courteous and modest, rather disposed to hear than to answer, given greatly to learning, weak and tender, but very comeful and bashful'[21] for one so young. Waterhouse thought Burghley would 'like of him as any that ever came within your charge'.[22] That would remain to be seen.

Robert was ten when his father died which made him the poorest earl in the kingdom as his grandfather Sir Francis Knollys called him. Walter had been in debt before his death and his will indicates £19,420 was still owed at the time of its writing. £10,000 had been borrowed from the queen to fund the Ulster campaign at 10 per cent interest and £6000 was yet to be repaid. £7000 was due to his creditors and another £6420 for the legacies under the will. Robert did however inherit Chartley Manor, the family home, where he had been living with his siblings.

Richard Broughton had been his tutor at Chartley and acted as Walter's lawyer, becoming trustee of the Devereux estates during Robert's minority. Thomas Ashton, previously headmaster of Shrewsbury School, founded by Royal Charter in 1552, who joined the Devereux household in 1571 and Robert Wright were also charged with his education. Accounts for 1577–1578 showed payments to tutors Robert and Edward Wright plus Piliard the Frenchman.

In January 1577 the young earl was sent to London as ward of court to live in Lord Burghley's household. According to the terms of Walter's will, his mother was required to move out of the family home and lived a somewhat peripatetic existence taking the younger children to visit their grandfather and friends before Penelope, Dorothy and young Walter were housed with their father's cousin the Earl of Huntingdon as their father had stipulated in his will. Robert however would join other young men in Lord Burghley's care.

Lord Burghley was Elizabeth I's closest advisor and Lord Treasurer as well as being Master of the Court of Wards, responsible for heirs of the peerage and landowners who had not reached their majority. As minors they could not yet hold their lands and so these reverted to the crown until these boys turned 21. Burghley was also responsible for his ward's education and marriages and to further their education established a school at Cecil House on the Strand.

Whilst here Essex would have met Lord Burghley's son Robert Cecil with whom he would have a tumultuous relationship in later years. Some historians have suggested that they vied for Lord Burghley's attention but their time together was relatively short and given Burghley was a busy man the time that he personally spent with the wards in his care was limited. He did however ensure a solid programme of education including Latin, French, writing, and Bible reading. And Lettice was pleased with her son's upbringing writing to Burghley 'thanks for the great goodness and fatherly love and friendship it pleaseth you to show my son, who may say he hath happily met with a second father instead of a guardian'.[23]

Robert left Cecil House in May when he was admitted to Trinity College, Cambridge. The Master of Trinity had been Dr John Whitgift, future Archbishop of Canterbury, someone Robert would come to know later in life. His position was passed on to John Still in 1577. Robert was only 11. Whilst this was not unusual, 15 was the recommended age as a younger boy was not thought to have 'good discretion how to govern himself there and moderate his expenses'.[24] Finance would not be the new earl's strong point.

Younger students had a private tutor to accompany them. Robert Wright went with Essex and by June was writing to Richard Broughton with a list of clothing that was urgently needed for the young earl before 'he shall not only be threadbare, but ragged'.[25] The funds were found not only to clothe him but to furnish his lodgings with glass for his windows, hangings for his study, tables, a footstool and a lock and three keys. His rooms were painted and shelving added. And then there were the books he needed for his first year of study including Isocrates in Greek, the *Chronicles of Holinshed*, *Questiones Bezae theologicae*, Ramus' logic and *Sturmius de Elocutione*. Robert's studies included rhetoric, logic, dialectic, philosophy, theology, mathematics, Greek and Hebrew.

Robert took his studies seriously and enjoyed his 'bookishnesse'[26] and there was still time to make the acquaintance of other young gentlemen such as Thomas White, Gabriel Montgomery, Gabriel and Richard Harvey, William Whitaker, John Overall and Hugh Broughton, brother of Richard Broughton. Robert was not always at Cambridge and often vacated his rooms for a trip to the countryside. When the plague arrived in 1578, he stayed at Keyston, a property left to him by his father, lived in by his uncle by marriage, Henry Clifford. Gabriel Montgomery, the son of the executed Count Montgomery, went with him for over six months.

In September of the same year Robert's mother officially married Robert Dudley, the Earl of Leicester, at Wanstead. They had secretly wed earlier in the year but when her father Sir Francis Knollys found out, he insisted another ceremony take place with witnesses. Given Leicester's previous affair with Lady Sheffield and her insistence they had married, the earl may have been in no position to marry Lettice. However Sir Knollys would not have let the ceremony go ahead if he felt the queen's favourite was truly contracted. As it was this was still a secret ceremony undertaken without Elizabeth's knowledge.

Leicester told his chaplain, Tyndall, that 'he had for a good season forborne marriage in respect of her Majesty's displeasure and that he was then for sundry respects and especially for the better quieting of his conscience determined to marry with the right honourable Countess of Essex'.[27]

The ceremony was performed on Sunday 21 September between seven and eight in the morning with Dudley's friends Lord North and the Henry Herbert, 2nd Earl of Pembroke, his brother Ambrose Dudley, and Richard Knollys, Lettice's brother, in attendance. Her father Francis led her to the altar. It is possible she was pregnant at the time but this is mostly contributed to the fact she wore a loose fitting gown. If she was the child did not survive.

Unaware of what had occurred, the queen arrived on Tuesday, at the end of her summer progress. A huge banquet was put on in her honour and although Lettice was probably present, the couple kept their recent nuptials quiet. Leicester may have thought keeping their new relationship from the queen would give him peace but he should have known better. Elizabeth always found out and her fury at those who married without her consent was terrible. When Katherine Grey married Edward Seymour without permission in 1560, and subsequently became pregnant, she asked Leicester for his help but he informed the queen. Katherine was sent to the Tower until 1563 and was kept in custody in private houses until her early death in 1568.

It is not known when Robert heard of his mother's remarriage but by 1579 it was the talk of the court. Although it was still a secret to all but family and he had surely been informed, the whispers had started. Whether he heard the rumours and felt the apprehension of those surrounding the queen when he attended the reception of the Duke of Casimir in the new year is hard to tell but he too knew it was only a matter of time before his sovereign found out that his mother had married the Earl of Leicester.

Elizabeth had been contemplating a marriage with the Duke of Alencon and the French ambassador Jean de Simier was sent to England to further his proposal. There was no love lost between the ambassador and the queen's favourite and when an assassination attempt was made on Simier's life, he blamed the Earl of Leicester. In a fit of spite he told the queen that her favourite had married Lettice.

Elizabeth was furious and flew into a rage. It was said the queen

intended to have (Leicester) committed to the Tower of London, which his enemies much desired. But the Earl of Sussex, though his greatest and deadliest adversary, dissuaded her. For he was of the opinion that no man was to be troubled with lawful marriage, which estate among all men hath ever been held in honour and esteem.[28]

Instead he was dismissed from court and sent to his home at Wanstead. There is a story that Elizabeth found Lettice and boxed her ears before banishing her. The queen had certainly struck her ladies before but whether true or not, Lettice was from now on unwelcome at court. Dudley stayed at Wanstead for some time telling Sir Christopher Hatton he was 'most unfit at this time to repair to that place where so many eyes are witnesses of my open disgrace delivered from her Majesty's mouth. Wherefor, if by silence it may be passed over (my calling for being but in general sort), I pray you let it be so'.[29]

Robert continued his studies away from the tension at home and at court. In October 1579 he met Gelly Meyrick, a Welshman, who would serve the earl throughout his life. He was also visited by Robert Rich, 3rd Baron Rich, who wanted to marry his older sister Penelope but was a bad influence on the young scholar taking Robert out of Cambridge without permission which led to Robert having to write Lord Burghley an apology for his 'honest pleasure'.[30] Rich may have disturbed his studies but in July 1581 he graduated as Master of Arts, aged 15.

Now free of university, the Earl of Essex spent time in London at Leicester House and Kenilworth, building on his relationship with his new stepfather. He may have also caught up with his mother and his new half-sibling, another Robert titled Lord Denbigh, who would affectionately be known as the 'noble imp' born 8 June 1581 at Leicester House.

His sister Penelope married Lord Rich in November of the same year. Their father Walter had wanted her to marry Philip Sidney, poet and scholar, writing to him on his deathbed of his wishes but it was not to be. Sidney would go on to marry Frances, Sir Francis Walshingham's daughter but he would regret his missed chance with Penelope and immortalise her as Stella in *Astrophel and Stella* (1591). But for now she would have to marry a man that was 'rough and uncourtly in manners and conversation, dull and uneducated'.[31] She had no wish to marry him but 'being in the power of her friends, was by them married against her will unto one against whom she did protest at the very solemnity and ever after'[32] and the marriage would always be an unhappy one. Robert however attended the ceremony in support of his sister but he cut a dash in lavish clothes that had cost him £40. His overspending was becoming an issue. Penelope returned to court to attend the queen after her marriage. Elizabeth may have still been furious with her mother but Penelope at least was welcome back.

Essex returned briefly to Cambridge to celebrate the queen's accession day on 17 November and then lived with his grandfather Sir Francis Knollys at Greys Court until February 1582. It was then decided to send him north to the Earl of Huntingdon, his sibling's guardian. Young Walter was still there and Robert doted on his little brother. It seems that there was still an issue with his finances and he wrote to Burghley in December 1582:

I hope your Lordship in courtesy will pardon my youth, if I have, through want of experience, in some sort passed the bounds of frugality. I cannot but embrace with duty your Lordship's good counsel, whose love I have effectively proved, and of whose care of my well doings I am thoroughly well persuaded. I do beseech your good lordship, not withstanding the lapse of my youth, still to continue a loving friend unto me, as I will acknowledge myself in all duty bound unto your Lordship.[33]

His sister Dorothy was also in trouble. Unbeknownst to Robert she had fallen in love with Thomas Perrot, son of Sir John Perrot, Lord Deputy of Ireland from 1584–1588 and reputedly the illegitimate son of Henry VIII, who lived near the Devereux country home in Lamphey, South Wales. Only Penelope knew of her sister's plans. They had obtained a licence in London and were secretly married at Broxbourne. The vicar had sensed something was afoot when a strange man asked him for the keys to the church which he refused. The strange man turned out to be the Perrot's family chaplain and once the door had been broken down, he married the couple whilst armed men stood on guard. Here was another marriage that the queen had not been asked permission for. Dorothy was one of her maids of honour and as such should have known her wrath especially after her reaction to her mother's marriage. Both Dorothy's new husband and his chaplain were sent to the Fleet prison until Burghley intervened.

Essex stayed with the Earl of Huntingdon until the end of 1583 and then joined his stepfather in London. When the Earl of Leicester went on his summer progress through the midlands the next year, he accompanied him visiting Buxton, Chester, Denbigh and Kenilworth, but their tour was cut short by the death of his half-brother, little Lord Denbigh in July at Wanstead.

Robert attended his funeral in August then left his mother and stepfather to their grief and retired to Lamphey, the Devereux Welsh estate. Here he did 'very honourably and bountifully keep house with many servants in livery and the repair of most gentlemen of those parts'.[34] His sister Dorothy and husband Tom were now living at nearby Carew Castle and often visited him. He seemed to be quite content to idle his time away but his mother was not happy at his lack of ambition. The letter she sent does not survive but his reply talks of her displeasure:

My very good Lady and mother
If I find by your Ladyship's displeasure conceived, that I am thought in sort to have offended, so I desire to deliver myself wholly, or in some part from the same fault. The which some will hardly term indutifulness to your Ladyship, others carefulness of mine own good, and many more think me inconsiderate, in not making your Ladyship more acquainted with my determinations. The name of undutifulness as a son I utterly abhor, my purposed course to do well I hope shall deliver me from the suspicion of carefulness of mine own estate, and if in your Ladyship's wise censure I be thought inconsiderate, I plead as a young man pardon for that fault whereto of all others our age is most subject [35]

He stayed at Chartley from April 1585 until August. In September he was staying in London with his step-father but had heard that Mary, Queen of Scots, was to be housed at his family home again.

He wrote to his grandfather Sir Francis Knollys who had been one of her keepers:

> *I am so much moved to think my poor and only house should be used against my will, that I make all the means I can to prevent any such inconvenience. The place which should be for the Queen of Scots is neither of strength nor pleasure, nor can any way fitly serve that turn, as many places in our country. And one reason which may persuade it to be spared is, that it is the only house of him which must, if that be taken, live at borrowing lodgings of his neighbours. I being wished to so many ill turns as the foregoing of the use of my house, the spoil of my wood, the marring of my little furniture, the miserable undoing of my poor tenants, I cannot but entreat my good friends to be a mean to the contrary, and, as a chief of them, your honourable self, whose help herein I humbly crave.*[36]

His grandfather did try to help by forwarding his letter to Sir Frances Walsingham with a note asking him to 'move Her Majesty to have some compassion of the miserable poor Earl of Essex' as he only had the one home. He also referred to his age when he said 'it is no policy for Her Majesty to lodge the Queen of Scots in so young a man's house as he is'.[37] But Mary would be moved to Chartley in late December 1585.

Robert, the new Earl of Essex, was presented to the queen at Nonsuch by the Earl of Leicester in September 1585 but he made little impact on the monarch and was just one of many young men who were introduced to her. She may have noticed his good looks and expensive clothes – he had borrowed £20 from Leicester to dress himself – but he was yet to impress her. The court was rife with the news of war in the United Provinces, now the Netherlands.

The queen appointed Leicester to lead the English troops to aid the Dutch against the Spanish and permission was granted for Robert to accompany him. Young Essex was eager for military glory but it also gave him an excuse to spend more money for which his grandfather soundly admonished him.

If I should not love you I should be unnatural; again, if I should flatter youthful humours in you, I should be guilty of the ruinous race of your undoing. Wherefore you must give me leave to say unto you, that wasteful prodigality hath devoured and will consume all noble men that be wilful in expenses before they have of their own ordinary living to bear out such wilful and wasteful expenses. You are so far off from being before hand in land and living left by your father to you, that by unhappy occasions your father hath not left you sufficient lands for to maintain the state of the poorest Earl in England; and also you are so far from goods and riches left upon you by your father, that you are left more in debt than one quarter of your land, to be sold by you, is able to discharge your debt.

Now, for you to put yourself to 1000l. charges (as I hear you have done, by borrowing reckonings vainly before hand), for your journey into the Low Countries, by levying and carrying with you a furnished band of men, needless and causeless; which band of men do also look to be recompensed with the spoil of your leases and livings; now if I should flatter you in this wasteful spoiling of yourself, then I should justly be accounted guilty of your ruinous race. I do like very well your desire to see the wars, for your learning; and do like your desire much the better, that you do take the opportunity of honouring my Lord of Leicester with your service under him; but this might have been done without any wasteful charge to yourself, for my Lord of Leicester doth set much by your company, but he delighteth nothing in your wasteful consumption.[38]

On 8 December Robert sailed from Harwich and arrived at Flushing two days later. His uncles William, Thomas and Francis were also amongst the contingent as well as his sister's husband Thomas Perrot. For Essex this was his first chance to shine and be damned what it cost him.

Lettice Knollys

Chapter Two

Essex's First Command

1586–1587

Increasing tensions across Europe made England fearful of a Spanish invasion. The Spanish Hapsburg Empire, under the rule of Phillip II, was trying to suppress Protestantism especially in the United Provinces where the Dutch were fighting for their independence. Elizabeth had a long history with Phillip who had been married to her older sister Mary. Once their relationship had been amicable enough – he had even supported her against her sister – but now she was queen, Philip's machinations were a threat.

Elizabeth had inherited a kingdom that had been divided over religion for many years. Her reign followed her father's break with Rome, her brother's fervent Protestantism and her sister's return to Catholicism. In order to bring peace to her realm Elizabeth and her councillors came up with the Religious Settlement. In 1559 the Act of Uniformity established The Book of Common Prayer and the Act of Supremacy underlined her role as supreme governor of the English church. A further act in 1563 laid out the doctrine of the Church of England. England would be protestant but Catholics would be tolerated.

Pope Pius V had excommunicated Elizabeth in 1570 as

the number of the ungodly hath gotten such power, there is now no place left in the whole World which they have not assayed to corrupt with their most wicked Doctrines: Amongst others, Elizabeth, the pretended Queen of England, a Slave of Wickedness, lending thereunto her helping hand, with whom, as in a Sanctuary, the most pernicious of all men have found a Refuge.

This very Woman having siezed on the Kingdom, and monstrously usurping the place of Supream Head of the Church in all England, and the chief Authority and Jurisdiction thereof, hath again brought back the said Kingdom into miserable destruction, which was then newly reduced to the Catholick Faith and good Fruit.[1]

But the papal bull also gave Catholics the order not to obey her on penalty of excommunication. It was supposed to support the nobles who had remained true to the old faith but Philip II, defender of the faith in Catholic Europe, believed the only way for England to return to the true religion would be by a full scale assault.

The Protestant Prince William of Orange, leader of the Dutch revolt, had been assassinated in 1584 and his people now looked to England for help. Elizabeth however was reluctant to become embroiled, preferring to try peaceful negotiation, even though those around her including the Earl of Leicester and Sir Francis Walsingham pressed her to send troops to their assistance. Not until the Siege of Antwerp in August 1585, when the Duke of Parma, appointed governor of the Spanish Netherlands by Philip II, led a Spanish force to capture the city, did Elizabeth relent. The Treaty of Nonsuch was drawn up promising 6400 soldiers, 1000 horse and 600,000 florins to support the cause and to send a 'gentleman of quality'[2] to aid governance. The Cautionary Towns of Brielle, Flushing and Fort Rammekens were to remain garrisoned by English troops as security. The gentleman of quality that Elizabeth chose was the Earl of Leicester. Sir Philip Sidney, Leicester's nephew, was to govern Flushing and Thomas Cecil, Burghley's eldest son, was to control Brielle.

Leicester was aging now and had not seen military service for 30 years but he believed that England's safety was tied to the security of the United Provinces. It was 'God's cause and her Majesty's'[3] that led him to his position of command. He raised

£25,000 for the campaign and was eager to engage the enemy. Unfortunately he would be pitted against the military strategy of the duke of Parma who was far more experienced.

Leicester was welcomed in the United Provinces as he rode with his stepson Essex and his personal retinue through Middleburg and north to Rotterdam, Delft, and the Hague in January. Everywhere they were feted as saviours and the queen of England was praised for sending such men to their aid. Each town tried to outdo another with lavish pageants, fireworks and feasting.

At the Hague Leicester accepted the title of governor-general of the United Provinces – a title Elizabeth had been repeatedly offered and refused. Essex was by his side with other nobles when Leicester was invested with great ceremony in the Great Hall of the Binnenhof. When Elizabeth heard she was furious and wrote to him:

> *How contemptuously we conceive ourselves to be used by you ... We could never have imagined (had we not seen it fall out in experience) that a man raised up by ourself and extraordinarily favoured by us, above any other subject of this land, would have in so contemptible a sort broken our commandment in a cause that so greatly toucheth us in honor...*[4]

She demanded he resign publicly but the Dutch were reluctant to be without such a leader and Elizabeth was wary of showing any discord to their enemies. Leicester would continue in the role until his command in the provinces was over.

Essex also had a new role when Leicester made him colonel-general of the horse on 10 January. It was a token appointment as Robert was untried and inexperienced in battle and Sir William Russell did the main work of organising the cavalry but it positioned Essex as a chief commander and Leicester's right-hand man.

They travelled on through Amsterdam and arrived at Utrecht. A magnificent St George's Day feast was celebrated with a chair kept for the queen. Although she was still furious at Leicester for becoming governor-general he maintained her presence as his sovereign. After a service at the cathedral, Essex escorted the dignitaries to the old Hall of the Knights of Rhodes for feasting and dancing. A joust was held and Robert took part in his first public display to show off his horsemanship skills and 'behaved himself so towardly that he gave all men great hope of his noble forwardness in arms'.[5]

In March, Essex left his stepfather for service in the field and was in a brief skirmish at Niekerken. The town of Grave had been relieved by English troops but was taken by the Duke of Parma who went on to seize Venlo and Nuys. Baron Hemart, who had been left in charge of Grave, was court martialled and Essex sat at his trial. Hemart, along with two of his captains, were executed for their failure to protect the town. This did nothing to boost the morale of the troops which was low and mutinous. The men had not been paid and many deserted but there was also trouble amongst the higher ranks. Leicester's men were divided between those who were loyal to the earl and those who were loyal to Sir John Norris, the colonel-general of the foot, who resented Leicester's authority.

Essex had been at a dinner when Norris' brother Edward was assaulted. After a night of continuous drinking, Count Hollock lost his temper and threw the lid of a wine bowl at the poor man's head cutting him severely. It prompted Essex to write to Leicester about trouble in the ranks 'I haste to write unto you, though I have no other advertisements but of our own private wars, which, I must needs think them more dangerous than the annoyance of any enemy...'.[6]

With fresh men and money from England, a new campaign saw the success of the capture of Doesburg on 2 September but Essex and his men still had to stop English soldiers from despoiling the town and its women. They travelled on towards Zutphen and Leicester sent ahead Essex, Sidney, Willoughby and Norris with 500 men to scout out the enemy and disrupt their supply line. The men rode into a dense fog and suddenly they were in the line of fire from 3000 Spanish infantry troops and 1500 cavalry. They had no choice but to charge into battle.

Sir Philip Sidney's horse was injured and he found another only to receive a musket shot in his thigh. The men wore cuisses for protection but Sir William Pelham, who had received a stomach wound at Doesburg, was unable to wear his and Sidney had left his own off in sympathy. Sidney was removed from the field and taken by barge to recover in the house of Mademoiselle Gruithuissens at Arnhem, where he was joined by his wife, Frances, the daughter of Sir Francis Walsingham. At first he appeared to be healing well but gangrene soon set in. Sidney knew he was dying and resigned to his fate had written his will but still he wrote to Jan Wier, physician to the Duke of Cleves, to come to his aid. It was too late. He died on 17 October mourned by all those who knew him. He was a star at the English court, diplomat, poet, soldier and courtier. Queen and country grieved for the loss of such a man. Leicester had lost his nephew and heir, a man he thought of as his son and devastated, wrote to Walsingham:

The grief I have taken for the loss of my dear son and yours would not suffer me to write sooner of those ill news unto you, especially being in so good hope so very little time before of his good recovery. But he is with the Lord and his will must be done. If he had lived, I doubt not but he would have been a comfort to us both, and an ornament to his house. What perfection he was grown unto and how able to serve her majesty and his country all men here almost wondered at. For mine own part, I have lost, beside the comfort of my life, a most principal stay and help in my service here and, if I may say it, I think none of all hath a greater loss than the Queen's majesty herself.[7]

Essex too greatly mourned his loss. Sidney had almost been his brother-in-law and was his cousin by marriage. The young earl looked up to him as a glowing example of an exemplary courtier and knight. Essex cherished Sidney's best sword left to him in his will. He was on the way to becoming like his idol when he was made knight-banneret, the highest rank of knighthood given on the battlefield, by Leicester.

The Battle of Zutphen marked the end of the campaign season and the Duke of Parma and his men retreated to winter quarters at Brussels whilst Essex returned to England in late October on the same black draped ship that carried Sidney's body. Leicester would follow him a few weeks later.

November 17 was always recognised as Elizabeth's Accession Day and great celebrations were held including a joust. This was the first time Essex performed in front of the queen and court. It may have been now that he used a blank shield with the motto 'par nulla figura dolori – nothing can represent my sorrow' to represent his grief over Sidney's death. He saw himself as Sidney's replacement – now he would be a chivalric knight, a hero of legend. His gift to the queen early next year would also represent himself and Sidney, a rainbow of diamond, opals and rubies sitting across twin pillars; one broken to represent the fallen hero and the other whole to represent himself.

When Leicester returned from the United Provinces at the end of November, Essex accompanied him to see the queen at Richmond. The queen was delighted to see her favourite returned safely and she desperately wanted his advice. Whilst he had been on campaign the Babington plot to free Mary Queen of Scots and place her on the throne was uncovered. The conspirators had been executed in October. Mary had been put on trial but Elizabeth could not bring herself to agree to her cousin's death. Knowing Leicester's influence with the queen, the privy councillors were also happy to see him back and wanted his support in getting the queen to agree to Mary's execution. Leicester was wholly behind the need to rid England of the Queen of Scots and over supper with Elizabeth he told her his thoughts. Essex was not yet high enough in Elizabeth's esteem to be a party to the discussion. He may have stayed at Leicester House or returned to Chartley from where Mary had been moved to Fotheringhay Castle in September.

Still Elizabeth delayed in signing Mary's death warrant until 1 February 1587. Changing her mind she asked for its recall but her councillors had taken matters into their own hands and seven days later Mary, Queen of Scots was executed. Elizabeth was furious but also clever. She knew the warrant would result in her cousin's death but this way she could place the blame on someone else, in this case, her unfortunate secretary Davison. He was sent to the Tower and Lord Burghley, who also felt her wrath, retired to the countryside for four weeks.

Essex made an attempt to help Davison by writing to the son of Mary, Queen of Scots, King James VI of Scotland 'Mr Davison, fallen into Her Majesty's displeasure and disgrace, beloved of the best and most religious in this land, doth stand as barred from any preferment or restoring in this place, except, out of their honour and nobleness of your royal heart, your Majesty will undertake his cause'.[8] But who was Essex to ask for leniency for the Queen's secretary? King James had no intention of helping the man who had shared responsibility for his mother's death nor of replying to Essex's letter. He had made an alliance with Elizabeth in July 1586 and was receiving £4000 from English coffers – a situation he wasn't about to upset.

Whilst Elizabeth was raging at those around her and crying for the loss of a fellow sovereign, Essex and Leicester attended Sidney's funeral along with 700 mourners in the old St Paul's Cathedral on 16 February 1587.

Sir Walter Raleigh, a prominent sailor, soldier, writer, poet and courtier wrote an epitaph for his fellow poet:

To praise they life, or wail thy worthy death,
And want thy wit, thy wit high, pure divine,
Is far beyond the power of mortal line,
Nor any one hath worth that draweth breath.

Yet rich in zeal, though poor in learning's lore,
And friendly care obscured in secret breast,
And love that envy in thy life suppressed,
They dear life done, and death hath doubled more.

And I, that in thy time and living state,
Did only praise they virtues in my thought,
As one that seld the rising sun hath sought,
With words and tears now wail they timeless fate.[9]

Raleigh had come to the queen's notice through his eagerness for adventure. In 1578, Raleigh sailed to America in command of the *Falcon*, one of seven ships equipped for the expedition by his half-brother Sir Humphrey Gilbert but bad weather forced them all back to port. Raleigh had at least managed to get as far as Cape Verde, off the coast of Africa, before returning home six months later. The voyage had not been a success but in 1584 the queen granted him his own patent for an expedition. Raleigh enlisted Philip Amadas and Arthur Barlow to command his ships. The English, under Raleigh's sponsorship, found the New World but it was to be a disaster. The first English settlers didn't have sufficient provisions to colonise Roanoke Island nor did they get on well with the native Indians. Disheartened, they returned home. Raleigh reported back to Elizabeth, intent on more exploration and named the land they had found, Virginia, in honour of the Virgin Queen.

Essex was becoming closer to the queen but at this stage he held no political sway nor influence over her. Elizabeth was happy to receive his attentions. He was one of a new generation of men including Walter Raleigh and Charles Blount who gave her pleasure. Her original favourites Leicester and Hatton were now aging and these younger men brought life to the court. Elizabeth was always one to bask in flattery and adoration and whereas once her favourites held ideas of marriage, now in her fifties, that possibility had died leaving her free to just enjoy their attentions.

By May Essex was one of the queen's closest companions. So much so that his servant Anthony Bagot told his father 'When she is abroad, nobody near her but my Lord of Essex and, at night, my Lord is at cards, or one game or another with her, that he cometh not to his own lodging till birds sing in the morning'.[10] His days were full of hunting, dancing, plays and masques.

The queen relied on him even more when the Earl of Leicester reluctantly returned to the United Provinces in June for the defence of Sluys and the queen gave Essex leave to stay in his stepfather's apartments. Leicester had helped to promote Essex to court and also organise his finances. In return Essex swore to look after Leicester's interest while he was away from court telling him 'I will watch with the best diligence I can that yowr enemies may not take advantage of your absence'.[11] Leicester had also put his stepson forward to take over his post of Master of the Horse, which came with a salary of £1500 a year, and this role would bring Essex even closer to the queen.

The court 'captured and stimulated men's imaginations, even if, eventually, it disheartened and disgusted them'[12] and it was not long before Essex had his first major falling out with the queen. During her summer progress she stayed at Northaw, the residence of the Earl and Countess of Warwick, where unbeknownst to Essex his sister Dorothy was staying.

Yesternight the Queen came to North Hall ... and knew my sister was in the house, she commanded my Lady of Warwick that my sister should keep her chamber... Her excuse was, first, she knew not of my sister's coming; and, besides, the jealousy that the world would conceive, that all her kindness to my sister was done for love of myself. Such bad excuses gave me a theme large enough, both for answer of them, and to tell her what the true causes were; why she would offer this disgrace both to me and my sister, which was only to please that knave Ralegh, for whose sake I saw she would both grieve me and my love, and disgrace me in the eye of the world.

From thence she came to speak of Ralegh; and it seemed she could not well endure any thing to be spoken against him; and taking hold of one word, disdain, she said there was no such cause why I should disdain him. This speech did trouble me so much, that, as near as I could, I did describe unto her what he had been, and what he was; and then I did let her know whether I had cause to disdain his competition of love, or whether I would have comfort to give myself over to the service of a mistress that was in awe of such a man. I spake, what of grief and choler, as much against him as I could, and I think he, standing at the door, might very well hear the worst that I spoke of himself. In the end, I saw she was resolved to defend him and to cross me. From thence she came to speak bitterly against my mother, which, because I could not endure to see me and my house disgraced (the only matter which both her choler and the practise of mine enemies had to work upon), I told her, for my sister she should not any longer disquiet her; I would, though it were almost midnight, send her away that night; and for myself, I had no joy to be in any place, but loth to be near about her, when I knew my affection so much thrown down, and such a wretch as Ralegh highly esteemed of her. To this she made not answer, but turned her away to my Lady of Warwick. So at that late hour I sent my men away with my sister; and after I came hither myself. This strange alteration is by Ralegh's means; and the Queen. That hath tried all other ways, now will see whether she can by those hard courses drive me to be friends with Ralegh, which rather will drive me to many other extremities.[13]

Essex was so enraged at the whole incident and the queen's attitude to him he rode to the coast to take ship. He decided he would follow his stepfather after all and take part in the defence of Sluys that was currently under siege but Elizabeth sent Robert Carey after him and all forgiven he acquiesced to turn back. The incident also highlighted his hatred of Raleigh who vied for the queen's attention. Essex had an innate jealousy of the men who surrounded the queen. He was a 'great resenter' and 'always carried on his brow either love or hatred and did not understand concealment'.[14] If he felt they were more favoured than he, given more gifts or assigned positions he craved, he would sulk for days on end.

But his hatred for Raleigh at this time was also underlined by the courtier's relationship with Leicester and Essex would make his stepfather's enemies his own. It had been rumoured that whilst they were in the United Provinces, Raleigh had been poisoning the queen against Leicester to the point that he was so worried about the rumours that Raleigh had written to the earl:

I have been of late very pestilent reported in this place to be rather a drawer back than a furtherer of the action where you govern. Your Lordship doth well understand my affection (feelings) towards Spain, and how I have consumed the best part of my fortune, hating the tyrannous prosperity of that estate, and it were now strange and monstrous that I should become an enemy to my country and my conscience.[15]

Raleigh asked Leicester to deal with him directly so that he would know the truth of any rumours. Whether Essex knew of this letter is not certain but if he did it did nothing to curb his animosity towards the adventurer. The Spanish ambassador even reported they had come to blows in August when Essex reportedly boxed Raleigh's ears. The situation worsened in September when Sir John Norris was recalled from the United Provinces to answer for his conduct towards Leicester. Raleigh took Norris' side 'ether of his ill nature or of emulation to the erlle of Essex'.[16]

Raleigh mourned Essex's rise and the loss of the queen's affection in his poem:

> Fortune hath taken thee away, my love,
> My life's joy and my soul's heaven above;
> Fortune hath taken thee away my princess,
> My world's delight and my true fancy's mistress.[17]

But there was some respite from the animosity when Leicester returned in December and Raleigh left court.

Robert Dudley, 1st Earl of Leicester

Chapter Three

The Spanish Threat

1588–1590

Early in 1588 the queen allowed Essex to reside at York House, one of the imposing mansions on the Strand, close enough to Leicester House for the young earl to see his stepfather regularly. Now at the age of 22 he was more independent and felt secure and in control of his destiny. Elizabeth had started to grant him lands and look on his requests with more favour. In April 1588 he was elected to become a knight of the garter, as his stepfather wished, and was never far from the queen's side. Things were going well for him.

But not so for England. The threat of war was looming when Philip II decided to enact his 'Enterprise of England' and send his armada of 130 ships, 19,000 men and 2500 guns to destroy the English fleet and follow it with a land invasion commanded by the Duke of Parma. In July Spanish ships were spotted at sea and warning beacons were lit along the coast. The English fleet were sent out to engage the Spanish under the command of Lord High Admiral Howard and Leicester was to command the land troops as lieutenant-general. Essex had been granted the position of general of the horse because the queen 'wold not have me discontented'[1] and had spent £3500 on his company of 320 harquebusiers, musketeers and light cavalry kitted out in the Devereux colours of tangerine and white to fight Spanish troops should they land in England.

On 27 July the Spanish anchored off the coast of Calais to wait for the Duke of Parma to join them by land. But Parma was delayed and that evening the English took the opportunity to send in eight fireships full of tar and pitch. Petrified of their ships going by in flames, the Spanish fleet scattered. English ships had blocked the channel so their flotilla, under the command of the Duke of Medina Sidonia, had to regroup further east.

On 29 July both fleets engaged in a nine hour battle close to Gravelines. Fierce gunshot bombarded the ships until a prevailing wind scattered the armada – said by some to be a 'Protestant' wind sent by God. The Lord Admiral chased them up to the Firth of Forth where he left them to the harsh navigation of Scotland and Ireland.

Unaware that the armada had been scattered, Queen Elizabeth made her famous speech to the 16,000 men at Tilbury on 9 August with Essex and Leicester in her entourage.

My loving people
We have been persuaded by some that are careful of our safety, to take heed how we commit our selves to armed multitudes, for fear of treachery; but I assure you I do not desire to live to distrust my faithful and loving people. Let tyrants fear. I have always so behaved myself that, under God, I have placed my chiefest strength and safeguard in the loyal hearts and good-will of my subjects; and therefore I am come amongst you, as you see, at this time, not for my recreation and disport, but being resolved, in the midst and heat of the battle, to live and die amongst you all; to lay down for my God, and for my kingdom, and my people, my honour and my blood, even in the dust.

I know I have the body of a weak, feeble woman; but I have the heart and stomach of a king, and of a king of England too, and think foul scorn that Parma or Spain, or any prince of Europe, should dare to invade the borders of my realm; to which rather than any dishonour shall grow by me, I myself will take up arms, I myself will be your general, judge, and rewarder of every one of your virtues in the field.

I know already, for your forwardness you have deserved rewards and crowns; and We do assure you on a word of a prince, they shall be duly paid. In the mean time, my lieutenant general shall be in my stead, than whom never prince commanded a more noble or worthy subject; not doubting but by your obedience to my general, by your concord in the camp, and your valour in the field, we shall shortly have a famous victory over these enemies of my God, of my kingdom, and of my people.[2]

Elizabeth did not know at this point that the Spanish commander had had no choice but to navigate the north coast of Scotland and continue down to the west coast of Ireland in a bid to reach home and safe shores. The Duke of Medina Sidonia thought they would be welcomed in Ireland, another Catholic country. Many ships, possibly 24, were wrecked along the rocky and treacherous west coast but those that landed discharged their battle worn and starving soldiers to be met by a hostile reception. Some 5000 soldiers were killed, some kept to ransom. It was punishable by death to harbour any of the Spanish sailors but some were spirited into barns and huts and integrated into the Irish community over the coming years.

With the loss of the armada the Duke of Parma refused to sail across the Channel without their support and the planned land invasion did not come to pass. What was left of the fleet returned to Spain thoroughly defeated. Half of their ships had been destroyed and more than 20,000 soldiers had lost their lives. The threat for now was over. Whilst Spain mourned their horrendous loss, celebrations were held across England and Essex was responsible for holding a military review at Whitehall to show off their finest troops. The earl paraded his company before the queen taking the opportunity to create a magnificent display. Dismounting from his horse Essex jousted against the Earl of Cumberland in a mock battle until the queen indicated they could stop. Disregarding her they continued to fight on, carried away with the moment, and Elizabeth now bored left them to it. Leicester, worn out from the past few days, watched from a nearby window.

So soon after England had celebrated its victory, Essex and Elizabeth were plunged into mourning when on 4 September the Earl of Leicester died. He had been on his way to Buxton to take the waters for his failing health and a reoccurring stomach complaint but fell ill at Cornbury, Oxfordshire. Before he died he wrote one last time to the queen, a letter she kept for the rest of her life.

I most humbly beseech your Majesty to pardon your poor old servant to be thus bold in sending to know how my gracious lady doth, and what ease of her late pains she finds, being the chiefest thing in this world I do pray for, for her to have good health and long life. For my own poor case, I continue still your medicine and find that (it) amends much better than with any other thing that hath been given me. Thus hoping to find perfect cure at the bath, with the continuance of my wonted prayer for your Majesty's most happy preservation, I humbly kiss your foot.[3]

Leicester was buried in the Beauchamp Chapel of the Church of St Mary the Virgin in Warwick, the same place as his son Lord Denbigh had been interred. Essex was chief mourner and headed the funeral procession of 100 people from Kenilworth to Warwick.

When Leicester died he was in debt for more than £50,000, half of it owed to the crown. The queen could finally get her revenge on Essex's mother Lettice by calling in the debt and seizing Kenilworth Castle and other lands. Goods from several of his houses were publicly auctioned. Lettice was residing at Drayton Basset when she was forced to leave due to a dispute over Leicester's will. Essex intervened asking one of his neighbours at nearby Chartley to assist the sheriff in removing one John Robinson from the house giving his mother a short reprieve.

Essex was left Leicester's best armour, two of his best horses and 'a George and Garter in the hope he shall wear it shortly'.[4] Leicester House had been left to the earl's illegitimate son and Essex now arranged to lease the house from him and in time he would change its name to Essex House where his sister Penelope would have her own apartments and all his family were welcome. He was closer than ever to the queen once she was out of mourning. It was even said he had won the hearts of his queen and the people. To keep him close Elizabeth had given him Leicester's old lodgings in Whitehall. But Essex hankered for more. He had risen so far but had plans to rise even further. Early in the year he had been incorporated with an honorary master of arts at Oxford to add to his degree from Cambridge. His hope was that as Leicester's death had left the position of Chancellor of Oxford vacant, it would be another role he could claim. The queen's favourite was dead and Essex wanted to fill his shoes. But Essex did not always get what he wanted and in this case Elizabeth granted the position to Sir Christopher Hatton.

The earl was becoming restless. He was secretly dealing with Sir Francis Drake, the infamous privateer and sea captain, to undertake a naval expedition. Although never far from court where 'the queen did fish for men's souls, and had so sweet a bait that no one could escape her network'[5] he wanted to be active and after his taste of military service in the United Provinces he pined for more.

His mounting frustration spilled over into his life at court. In November 1588 he became jealous of Charles Blount, another young courtier, who had been gifted a golden chessman from the queen for his outstanding performance at the tilt. Blount pinned the chessman to his sleeve with a red ribbon making Essex comment 'Now I perceive every fool must wear a favour'.[6] The offended Blount challenged Essex to a duel at Marylebone Park where the earl was injured in the thigh by Blount's rapier. Duelling was forbidden and when the queen heard she banned them both from court to cool down but commented 'By God's death it was fit that someone or other should take him down and teach him better manners, otherwise there would be no rule with him'.[7] The queen had already seen how Essex liked to overreach himself and was not impressed. However it amused her to have two young bucks fighting over her but when Essex challenged Raleigh to a duel later in the year she ordered the privy council to put a stop to it. Whereas Essex's relationship with Raleigh would always be tenuous, the earl would become great friends with Blount and often entertain him at Essex House where it became a meeting place for his sister Penelope and Blount when they became lovers.

At the beginning of 1589 Essex was in debt for £23,000 but nevertheless presented Elizabeth with a new year's gift of a jewel of a naked man inside a flower of gold. Neither his grandfather, the Earl of Huntingdon or Leicester had ever managed to curb his excessive spending but in January the queen granted him the right to gather tax on sweet wines renewable every five years, once the right of his stepfather. It was a great boost to his income but he still wanted more.

Although Essex received benefits from Leicester's death he would never truly supplant him in the affections of the queen. He would never become her 'eyes' as his stepfather had been and she would never give him a nickname of endearment although she sometimes called him Robin. Still she wanted him close by and refused his request to join an expedition to Spain and Portugal commanded by Sir Francis Drake and Sir John Norris. He irritated and infuriated her but he also entertained her and somewhat filled the gap in her life created by Leicester's death.

The exiled Don Antonio de Crato, had urged Queen Elizabeth to support his claim to the Portuguese throne, now controlled by the Spanish, and insisted those that helped would obtain great riches. Elizabeth agreed to send six ships and invested £60,000 in the expedition but she was adamant that Essex was not to go.

The earl had other ideas and on 3 April he left London after writing forty farewell letters to his family and friends. To his grandfather he wrote:

> *What my state now is, I will tell you: my revenue no greater than when I sued my livery; my debts at the least two or three and twenty thousand pounds; Her Majesty's goodness hath been so great I could not ask more of her; no way left to repair myself but mine own adventure...*[8]

Essex rode 220 miles in three days reaching Falmouth where his trusted friend Sir Roger Williams, a seasoned soldier who had served under Leicester in the United Provinces, was waiting on the *Swiftsure*. They set sail immediately avoiding the other ships whilst Drake and Norris made for Cadiz. Essex was unaware that Elizabeth had sent men down to the coast to retrieve him as soon as she found out he was missing but he knew she would order his recall once she found him gone. Failing any sight of him letters were sent to Drake and Norris ordering his immediate return but the *Swiftsure* did not join the fleet until 13 May and by then the winds were against him. Drake wrote to the queen that Essex had been informed of his need to turn back for England but due to the winds and not being able to 'spare out of the fleet a ship of so good service as the Swiftsure'[9] he was unable to.

Essex was more than ready to see action and arriving at the fort of Peniche he 'was the first that landed, who, by reason the billows were so great, waded to the shoulders to come ashore'.[10] Following him was his brother Walter, who had recently married Margaret Dakins (later Lady Margaret Hoby) and his companion Sir Roger Williams and their men who soon overcame the garrison and took the town.

Their next objective was to take Lisbon; Norris commanding his troops over land and Drake approaching by sea. Reaching the suburbs, they found the inhabitants had retreated behind their city walls. The troops were starving, tired and dejected but were told not to plunder the Portuguese and kept to their command. Taking a well-earned rest they were attacked by Spaniards. When fierce fighting broke out Essex was in the thick of the fray. Don Antonio, sent men to aid the attack but it wasn't enough. Forced to retreat Essex brought up the rearguard and in a final gesture shoved his pike through the city gates 'demanding aloud if any Spaniard mewed therein durst adventure forth in favour of his mistress to break a lance'.[11] There was no answer.

The English retreated to Cascaes and Essex 'commanded all his stuff to be cast out of his carriages and to be laden with sick men and gentlemen that fainted'.[12] At the small coastal town Norris goaded the Spanish to attack them. Essex sent word he would match any of their challengers but again there was no answer. Whilst at Cascaes Drake was able to plunder 60 ships laden with goods. Their expedition may have failed but at least there was something to show for it. Supply ships arrived and with it a letter from the queen written to him on 15 April but not received until June:

Essex – Your sudden and undutiful departure from our presence and your place of attendance, you may easily conceive how offensive it is, and ought to be, unto us. Our great favours bestowed on you without deserts, hath drawn you thus to neglect and forget your duty; for other constructions we cannot make of these your strange actions. Not meaning, therefore, to tolerate this your disordered part, we gave directions to some of our Privy Council to let you know our express displeasure for your immediate repair hither; which you have not performed, as your duty doth bind you, increasing greatly thereby your former offence and undutiful behaviour, in departing in such sort without our privity, having so special office of attendance and charge near our person. We do therefore charge and command you forthwith, upon receipt of these our letters, all excuses and delays set apart, to make your present and immediate

repair unto us, to understand our farther pleasure. Whereof see
you fail not, as you will be loth to incur our indignation, and will
answer for the contrary at your uttermost peril.[13]

It was now time for Essex to return home and answer to the
queen but Elizabeth had already forgiven her errant boy and
he was welcomed back into her favour. Raleigh had had the
opportunity to spend more time with his sovereign but he
was no match for the queen's new favourite. Essex's return
pushed Raleigh out of the limelight and it was rumoured the
earl 'hath chassed Mr Rauly from the coart and hath confined
him to Irland'.[14] Raleigh laughed it off saying he was content to
return to his Irish estate in Youghal near Cork, given to him by
the crown, where he had settled 144 Englishmen and said it was
sorely in need of management.

In the autumn Essex began to write to King James VI of
Scotland again as did his sister Penelope, including a portrait
of herself. His aim could only have been to inveigle himself
with a possible contender to the succession. James was not
overly concerned by their letters and regarded 'not their offers
much'.[15] Burghley was informed of the correspondence by his
man at James' court which saw Essex sternly reprimanded by
the queen. She may have been favouring him more but she did
not want him meddling in Scottish affairs. There were men far
more experienced than he, like her trusted secretary, who could
deal with the king of Scotland.

Essex's mother Lettice had not heard from him in some time
and wanted to know the latest news from her son. Still banned
from court she wrote to him in December:

Your poor friends here, my dear son, are in great longing to know
how you fare, to which purpose we have addressed this bearer to
bring us true word thereof. For although our ears are fed with many
flying reports, yet we believe nothing but what we receive from the

oracle of truth, wherefore relive us, if it please you, with some of your occurents.[16]

She had remarried Sir Christopher Blount in July – a man 16 years younger than her who had served under Leicester and was his Gentleman of the Horse. Essex had thought it an 'unhappy choyse'[17] but Blount would prove to be a faithful companion. Essex had not seen his mother for some time as 'the queen hath stayed me here'[18] but in March he was negotiating with his mother to lease Wanstead to him, urged on by Elizabeth, and wrote to Lettice 'Though I confess I do greatly affect it, yet I will not desire it so as your ladyship shall lose one penny profit or one hour of pleasure that you may have there'.[19]

Essex made his own choice to marry in the following month and again this was a marriage that the queen was to be unaware of for months. The earl married Sir Philip Sidney's widow, Frances not long after the death of her father Sir Francis Walsingham, Elizabeth's greatest spymaster. Walsingham had died in debt although Frances had been granted a £300 annuity. It was a significant sum of money to bring to a marriage that does not appear to have been a love match. Some said the earl had promised Sir Philip Sidney to look after his wife and daughter as he lay dying. If so Essex had certainly taken his time. Of course when the queen found out she was furious but her anger soon abated. What she didn't know was that not only was Frances pregnant but so was Essex's mistress, Elizabeth Southwell, a maid of honour to the queen.

By June Essex was feeling the pinch of his financial strain again when the queen called in her debt forcing him to sell the manor of Keyston.

He wrote to her:

As in love there can be nothing more bitter than unkindness, so than that there is no truer a touchstone of an humble and constant faith. Since it pleaseth your Majesty to try me with what duty and patience I can bear the hard measure that is offered me, I will humbly crave pardon to tell your Majesty without offence, what sense I have of it. When it pleased your Majesty to send me word you would forebear the 3000l. for six months longer, your kindness in it was a greater satisfaction to my mind than the loan of so much money could be a benefit to my purse; and now that your Majesty repents yourself of the favour you thought to do me, I would I could, with the loss of all the land I have, as well repair the breach which your unkind answer hath made in my heart as I can with the sale of one poor manor answer the sum which your Majesty takes of me. Money and land are base things, but love and kindness are excellent things, and cannot be measured but by themselves. Therefore I will not charge your Majesty refusing me so small a matter, nor tell you that you once promised it; but I will assure you that I will owe you all duty for ever, and I must needs love you till I be discouraged.[20]

He may have had to sell his property but he had no qualms in letting the queen know he was unhappy about it. Their correspondence would chart the ups and downs of their relationship and neither would hold back when chastising the other.

Essex made some effort to atone for his marriage and perceived sins (so he felt) on this year's Accession Day. It was a special occasion celebrating the retirement of the Queen's Champion, Sir Henry Lee but Essex certainly lowered the mood by entering on a chariot pulled by coal black horses as part of a funeral cortege.

Then proudly shocks amid the Martiall throng,
Of lustie Lancieres, all in Sable sad,
Drawen on with cole-blacke Steeds of duskie hue,
In stately Chariot full of deepe deuice,
Where gloomie Time sat whipping on the teame,

Iust backe to backe with this great Champion;
Yoong Essex, that thrice honorable Earle,
Yclad in mightie Armes of mourners hue,
And plume as blacke as is the Rauens wing,
(peele Polyhymnia)[21]

He may have lowered the tone but Essex was fast becoming a patron of the arts and a poet himself. Books one to three of Edmund Spenser's *Faerie Queene* were published this year and contained a dedication to the earl as well as other nobles including Sir Christopher Hatton, Burghley, the Earls of Oxford, Northumberland and Cumberland, Lord High Admiral Charles Howard, Sir Francis Walsingham and Sir Walter Raleigh. Raleigh added a poem of his own to which Essex took offence and shot off his own poem in retaliation likening his nemesis to a cuckoo, parrot and an ass.

Muses no more, but mazes be your names
When discord's sound shall mar your concord sweet
Unkindly now your careful fancy frames,
When fortune treads your favours under feet;
But foul befall that cursed cuckoo's throat
That so hath crossed sweet Philomela's note.

And all unhappy hatched was that bird,
That parrot-like can never cease to prate;
But most untimely spoken was that word,
That brought the world in such a woeful state
That love and liking quite are overthrown
And in their place are grief and sorrows grown.

Is this the honour of a haughty thought,
For honour's hate to have all spite at love?
Hath wretched skill this reason taught,

In this conceit such discontent to move,
That beauty is so of herself bereft,
That no good hope of aught good hap is left?

Oh let no phoenix look upon a crow,
Nor dainty hills bow down to dirty dales;
Let never heaven an hellish humour know,
Nor firm affect give ear to foolish tales;
For this in fine will fall to be the troth,
That filthy water makes unwholesome broth.

Woe to the world, the sun is in a cloud,
And darksome mists do overrun the day;
In high conceit, is not content allowed;
Favour must die and fancies wear away.
O heavens, what hell! The bands of love are broken,
Nor must a thought of such a thing be spoken.

Mars must become a coward of his mind,
Whiles Vulcan stands to prate of Venus' toys.
Beauty must seem to go against her kind,
In crossing nature in her sweetest joys;
But oh, no more, it is too much to think,
So pure a mouth should puddle-water drink.

But since the world is at this woeful pass,
Let love's submission honour's wrath appease.
Let not a horse be mated with an ass,
Nor hateful tongue an happy heart disease;
So shall the world commend a sweet conceit,
And humble faith on heavenly favour wait.[22]

Essex would always try to have the last word.

Defeat of the Spanish Armada

Chapter Four

The French Campaign

1591–1592

In January 1591 Essex became a father when Frances gave birth to his son also named Robert. His mother Lettice stood as godmother at his baptism in St Olave's Church, not far from the Tower of London, with his grandfather Sir Francis Knollys and Penelope's husband, Lord Rich as godfather. But his thoughts were far from family life.

Henri of Navarre had become king of France in 1589 after the assassination of Henri III. He was a Protestant and as such was not recognised by his Catholic subjects as king. The Catholic League, backed by Spanish troops, rejected his sovereignty and Henri IV was fighting to gain control of France. Elizabeth had sent Lord Willoughby over to assist him with money and men but the king was still in difficulty. His general Turenne arrived in England in November 1590 to ask for more assistance but as always Elizabeth was wary about becoming embroiled in hostile disputes. However if Spain controlled France and its ports the threat of another invasion was all too likely.

Essex on the other hand was eager to prove his worth and ally with France against the Spaniards. He welcomed Turenne and provided accommodation and entertainment and more importantly funds for him to continue the war. After Essex's foray in the United Provinces he was eager for military action and kept up a correspondence with the king of France, assuring him of his fidelity and informing him of how anxious he was to join him writing 'there is nobody in the world who hates the name of unfruitful more than I, or who feels more envious of those who can be more forward in your service'.[1] At the same time he was begging Elizabeth to let him go to France. He was determined to take his first military command and the French knew he was eager to accommodate them. On 9 April 1591 the earl entertained the French ambassador, Beauvoir la Nocle, to the cost of £53 at Wanstead and assured him of his assistance. His sister Penelope accompanied him as host eager to support him. He had even gone so far as to buy the governorship of Alderney, one of the Channel Islands, the previous year as a base from which to enter France. Penelope and her husband Lord Rich had either loaned or given him the £1600 he paid for a 1000 year lease on the island, castle and its contents.

Elizabeth was not ready to give Essex any command yet. Sir John Norris was sent with 3000 men to assist the beleaguered king of France. The earl's friend Sir Roger Williams took command of 600. It must have galled Essex that he was not allowed to go. Still he curried Burghley and Hatton's support and eventually the queen was persuaded to give him his first military command after he spent two hours on his knees begging for the commission. He wrote triumphantly to Richard Bagot 'I am commanded into France for the establishing of the brave King in quiet possession of Normandy' and asked him to send on 'tall men well horsed, or good horses or geldings'[2] by 10 July to join his company. He was officially ordered to lead the support force in Normandy on 21 July and paraded his troops at Covent Garden in their orange and white Devereux liveries before the queen. But Elizabeth was no fool when it came to sending Essex off on his own and she tasked other more senior and experienced men to guide her over-zealous favourite. Sir Thomas Leighton and Sir Henry Killigrew would advise him on military strategy and Sir Henry Unton, the new English ambassador to France, was in effect Essex's minder and would report on his actions to Burghley.

The queen also informed Henri IV of Essex:

If, which most I fear, the rashness of his youth does not make him too precipitate, you will never have cause to doubt his boldness in your service, for he has given too frequent proofs that he regards no peril, be it what it may, and you are entreated to bear in mind that he is too impetuous to be given the reins. But, my God, how can I dream of making any reasonable requests to you, seeing you are so careless of your own life. I must appear a very foolish creature, only I repeat to you that he will require the bridle rather than the spur.[3]

Essex landed at Dieppe on 2 August with around 4000 men. It seems he had left without saying goodbye to his wife who wrote to him of her sadness of his 'going away without taking leave of me'.[4] But Essex had other things on his mind. Elizabeth had been very clear on his mission. They were to relieve the siege of Rouen removing the threat of a Catholic controlled north coast and assist Henri IV's troops to take command.

Essex was eager to appease his queen and immediately sent despatches to Elizabeth including:

I must not let this second day pass without complaining to your Majesty of the misery of absence. I shall think my life very unpleasant till I have rid myself of this French action, that I may once again enjoy the honor, the pleasure, the sweetness which your presence is accompanied with. That business which we would fain have ended, we go about in haste. By those whom I meet upon the way, I hear that our action ripens apace. I hope your Majesty shall presently have great honor by the service of your little troop; and I, as a reward of my service, to be soon at home at your Majesty's feet, whence nothing but death, or your inconstancy, which is not in rerum natura, can drive me. Never be it heard or seen that your Majesty be less than the greatest, the healthfullest, or the happiest, or other than a most gracious kind lady to your Majesty's humblest, faithfullest, and most affectionate servant.[5]

Henri IV was not there to meet him with his forces and Essex had to wait until Sir Roger Williams arrived with a message and invitation from the king. Against Elizabeth's wishes the earl and a detachment of his men had to travel four days to Compiegne skirting through enemy territory and the besieged town of Rouen to the detriment of Essex's men as the 'journey was so hard, that it hath destroyed divers young soldiers'.[6] Yet Essex managed a glorious entrance at his meeting with Henri

> *he had before him six pages mounted on chargers and dressed in orange velvet all embroidered with gold. And he himself had a military cloak of orange velvet covered all with jewels...his dress and furniture on his horse alone were worth sixty thousand crowns. He had twelve tall body-squires and six trumpets sounding before him.*[7]

Essex was royally entertained but Elizabeth was furious with this delay and she asked the king of France, 'Do you really think, mon frere, that these are the ways to treat a prince who allows her subjects to risk their lives to defend your kingdom?'[8] Her troops should have been at Rouen with the French army but Henri had other ideas. He still did not return to the city but headed to Germany for reinforcements leaving Essex to ride hard for Dieppe to re-join the body of his troops through countryside rife with hostile soldiers under the command of Villars, the Catholic League's governor of Rouen. In Dieppe the troops were becoming increasingly ill with dysentery and malaria.

Elizabeth waited at Portsmouth for five days after sending instructions that Essex tell Henri IV she requested an audience. The earl received no such command and whilst Elizabeth heard reports of his gallivanting across the French countryside with Henri IV nowhere in sight her fury grew.

She wrote to Essex of her displeasure and for him 'being more plyable to a strange king's demaunds then to his soveraigne's instructions'[9] but Essex was in a world of pain. Not only had he fallen ill with a fever but his younger brother Walter had taken a detachment of 1200 men to Rouen on 8 September and had been fatally wounded by a musket shot. Essex spiralled into a deep depression and could hardly rise from his bed. This was not the glorious military action of his first command he had foreseen but a tragic and debilitating time in his life.

He wrote to Robert Cecil, 'I was punished with a fever, and my heart broken with the Queen's unkindness. Since the writing of my last, I lost my brother in an unfortunate skirmish before Rouen. I call it unfortunate that robbed me of him who was dearer to me than ever I was to myself'.[10]

The queen had sent troops to rescue Rouen from the enemy which had not happened. Her costs were mounting and the Spaniards were still a threat so in September she issued a statement 'A Declaration of the Causes that move her Majesty to revoke her forces in Normandy' in which she recalled Essex and his troops. But the earl was not done yet and finally Henri's forces under the command of Marshal Biron took Gournay-en-bray on 27 September supported by English troops. This would not be the first time he would ignore a direct order.

At the beginning of October he knighted 24 men – another move that would infuriate the queen. His commission had specifically instructed him 'not to bestow the honour of knighthood, or of arms, on any person of mean birth, or not deserving the same'.[11] During her reign Elizabeth had curbed the amount of knighthoods given out and was loath to see more created especially those she had not considered and approved herself.

He returned briefly to England and the queen made her displeasure felt in person. He wrote to her of his poor reception 'I see your Majesty is constant to ruin me; I do humbly and patiently yield to your Majesty's will. I appeal to all men that saw my parting from France, or the manner of my coming hither, whether I deserved such a welcome or not. To be full of words when a man is full of affliction, is for him that is not resolved what to do with himself'.[12] Then she decided to send him back. When he reached Dieppe he found his army decimated by half through illness and desertion. Yet these few men joined in the siege of Rouen on 11 November when Essex issued a challenge of single combat to Villars, to decide 'the king's quarrel is juster than the League's, that I am better than you, and my mistress is fairer than yours'.[13] Villars declined the challenge.

Finally the queen was happy enough with Essex's conduct to tell him he could now return home but no sooner was he back in England then news reached them that Spanish troops were being reinforced by the Duke of Parma's men. He returned but it was obvious the siege was failing. Even more men had fallen ill and Essex 'sent away with passport as many as were able to creep towards Dieppe on their feet'.[14]

Elizabeth had run out of patience and wrote Essex a terse letter:

We hear besides to our no small wonder, how little the King regards the hazards of our men, and how you, our General, at all times refuse not to run with them to all service of greatest peril, but even, like the forlorn hope of a battle, to bring them to the slaughter. And therefore in regard that divers gentlemen of good quality, dear to their parents and blood, should not be vainly consumed to the grief of such as were contented to suffer them to go there for our service, we do command you to send them back although yourself should stay; which for our own part, notwithstanding daily entreating to revoke you, we are determined not to do so long as one man is left behind; only this we are content to let you know, that if at last you shall be so well advised as to think how dishonourable it is for you to tarry with so mean a charge, after so many men consumed so little to the purpose they were sent for, with many other absurd defects, which blemish the honour of the place you hold under us as our General, we shall right well allow of your judgment to return

as a thing very fit and necessary to be performed, and hereby do
authorise you to leave our said companies with the Marshal and
Serjeant Major, without putting Sir Thomas Leighton to any
further trouble in this hard time of winter, so great an enemy to his
infirmity; of which our pleasure, leaving other particularities to be
answered by our Treasurer, we have thought good to acquaint you
by our own handwriting.[15]

The winter season was upon them and Essex withdrew but not before issuing another personal challenge to Villars that was declined. As he boarded his ship he dramatically drew his sword and kissed it.

During Essex's absence his mistress Elizabeth Southwell gave birth to the earl's illegitimate son Walter who would join his grandmother Lettice at her household in Drayton Basset. Queen Elizabeth had no idea Essex was the father or her wrath would have been great. Thomas Vavasour took the blame and was imprisoned for the deed.

Instead the earl received a joyous welcome home and even Elizabeth was allowed to return to court. His return to England in January 1592 also saw the birth of his legitimate second son, also called Walter, who was not to live long. Essex was back in Elizabeth's good graces. Yet as before Elizabeth would not give him everything he wanted. He had coveted the position of Chancellor of Oxford University made vacant by the death of Sir Christopher Hatton but this position she gave to Lord Buckhurst instead.

Sir Robert Naunton later tried to explain the queen's relationship with Essex in his *Fragmenta Regalia, or Observations on the late Queen Elizabeth, her Times and Favourites.* The queen certainly allowed him liberties and Essex reciprocated with extremes of adoration and anger.

Naunton saw the reason as being 'a violent indulgence of the Queen which is incident to old age when it encounters with a pleasing and suitable object...' but felt there was

a fault in the object of her grace, my Lord himself, who drew in too fast like a child sucking on an over-uberous nurse; and had there been more decent decorum observed in either of these, without doubt the unity of their affections had been more permanent, and not so in and out as they were, like an instrument ill tuned and lapsing to discord.[16]

However Essex settled into life back at court and resided in Leicester House now renamed Essex House. The earl was always on the lookout for those who could be of use to him and during 1591 Francis Bacon, a barrister and MP, became his adviser. Francis and his brother Anthony were the sons of Sir Nicholas Bacon, Lord Keeper of the Great Seal, who had died in 1579 and Lord Burghley was their uncle. When Anthony returned to England in February 1592 after travelling abroad and visiting the courts of Europe he first went to Burghley for employment as his brother had done before him but the elderly statesman turned both of the siblings down. Now they saw a way to further themselves by aligning themselves with Essex and the earl saw how useful these men could be in establishing an intelligence network to rival Burghley's.

Francis had already made a start by contacting Thomas Phelippes, Walsingham's chief codebreaker who would also bring with him other agents from the old intelligence network that the Bacon brothers could use in service to the earl. He told Phelippes

I send you a copy of the letter I have written to the Earl, touching the matter proposed between us, wherein you will see how I have spoken of you. I advise you, in this beginning of intelligence, to spare no pains. The more plainly and frankly you deal with the Earl in this action, the better.[17]

Anthony was not a well man, acutely suffering from gout, but he had outstanding contacts having previously worked for Walsingham and was well placed to manage a network of secret agents to inform Essex of political manoeuvres and intrigues. He became his secretary in charge of foreign correspondence and began an intelligence service to rival that of the Lord Chancellor.

Essex knew Lord Burghley and his son Robert had the queen's ear and much more influence over her decisions. By setting up his own network he hoped the queen would take him more seriously, see that he had grown from the rash young man he had been and was willing to work for his queen and country. He saw a need to move from military pursuits to influencing politics. While his rivalry with the Cecil's would never break down to open hostility he would use his influence to try and circumvent theirs. Although he had spent some of his childhood with the Cecil's he saw them as rivals for the queen's attention – something he felt, albeit unrealistically – should be his alone.

Strangely Essex overcame his resentment towards Raleigh who had secretly married one of Elizabeth's ladies, Bess Throckmorton, and was godfather to his son Damerei born in the spring. The men had found common ground in 1591 over their dislike of the persecution of certain Puritans. The case of John Udall, the compiler of the first Hebrew dictionary in English, who was sentenced to death for treason had stunned them and Phelippes wrote 'The Puritans hope well of the Earl of Essex, who makes Raleigh join him as an instrument from them to the Queen, upon any particular occasion of relieving them'.[18] Their intervention stopped his sentence from being carried out but Udall later died in prison.

Essex was also friends with Bess's brother Arthur Throckmorton who was concerned that when the queen found out about her marriage to Raleigh and the birth of their son they would both need supporters at court. The earl may have shared his concerns but on the other hand knowing Elizabeth's severe displeasure was inevitable, could predict Raleigh's downfall. By June Raleigh and Bess were in the Tower of London and Essex's rival would be out of favour for five years.

Sir Walter Raleigh

Chapter Five

The Lopez Plot

1593–1594

London had been rife with plague over the winter of 1592 and into the New Year. It would continue to decimate lives throughout 1593. The theatres were closed and gatherings curtailed in a bid to curb the spread of the disease but the death toll continued to rise. Those that could moved out of the city to the cleaner atmosphere of the countryside. Essex's men Anthony and Francis Bacon continued to run his intelligence network from Gorhambury, the Bacon family home, and Twickenham Park, leased by their half-brother Edward Bacon. Essex needed to stay close to the queen. Parliament was due to open in February and he had been angling for a position on the Privy Council. The earl felt it was time he was taken more seriously and his worth rewarded.

And the queen must have seen her favourite growing into a valuable statesman as she agreed to advance him to privy councillor. Finally he could sit alongside Burghley and his son Robert amongst others. He would now have a voice at the highest level. One courtier commented 'His Lordship is become a new man, clean forsaking all his former youthful tricks, carrying himself with honourable gravity, and singularly liked of both in Parliament and at the Council table for his speeches and judgement'.[1] Although his reputation was bolstered, his advisor Francis was about to lower his.

Elizabeth needed more money in her Treasury and the aim of Parliament was to approve a series of levies to raise funds. The French campaign had cost the state much and the threat from Spain was still there, requiring more funds should they need to undertake further action.

Bacon gave a speech in parliament that would enrage the queen and impede his career prospects. He agreed subsidies must be collected but not within the six years or under as suggested.

For impossibility, the poor man's rent is such as they are not able to yield it and the general commonalty is not able to pay so much upon the present. The gentlemen, they must sell their plate and the farmers their brass pots before this will be paid. And for us, we are here to search the wounds of the realm and not to skin them over, wherefore we are not to persuade ourselves of their wealth more than it is.

The danger is this, we breed discontent in the people, and in a cause of jeopardy her Majesty's safety must consist more in the love of her people than in their wealth, and therefore not to give them discontent in paying these subsidies.[2]

After this the queen refused to talk to Bacon or even allow him to come into her presence. Bacon told Lord Burghley 'I was sorry to find that my last speech in Parliament, delivered in discharge of my conscience and duty to God, Her Majesty, and my country, has given offence'.[3] But he did not apologise. Much like his master.

And Lord Burghley was not so convinced that Essex was a changed man either. He was well aware of the intelligence network that was operating. Several of his own men had gone over to the earl but he also knew that Essex was still corresponding with King James of Scotland and was determined to monitor his letters.

Essex had actually charged Anthony Bacon with continuing his correspondence with Scottish agents and Anthony had contacts of his own to utilise. He had met Dr Thomas Moresin whilst in France and on his return to Scotland Bacon acquired his services to report on the goings on at the court of James VI.

The queen and her council feared that Scotland would make an alliance with Spain and Moresin's despatches were so important 'the queen did never take more satisfaction in any man's service'.[4] She was satisfied with Essex's espionage and tasked him to write 'a draft of an instruction for a matter of intelligence'.[5]

In June the Catholic spy Anthony Standen arrived back in London. He had served Mary Queen of Scots until she was executed when he fled to Spain. Philip II had used his services for a while until Walsingham employed him to spy on the Spanish and report on the Armada. He had been arrested in Bordeaux and imprisoned until Bacon arranged his release, Walsingham being dead and no longer able to help his agents. Standen had already been sending correspondence about the Spanish to Bacon and Essex but his news was old and when Essex passed his letters on to the queen she derided him for his out-of-date information. Now he had returned to English soil Standen sought a place in Burghley's service but it was Bacon who pressed him to work for Essex, placing a gold medallion around his neck.

Another man who entered Essex's employ in 1593 was Don Antonio Perez. Perez had once been King Phillip of Spain's secretary. He had been responsible for the murder of Escovedo, Don John of Austria's secretary, for which he was imprisoned for 11 years until he escaped to France. Now he had arrived in England willing to relay Spanish intelligence.

A letter Essex sent to Phelippes asked him to find out more about Perez.

The informer must be extraordinary careful in getting all the news he can of Antonio Perez, what is the end of his coming hither, and how he has been dealt with. He may advertise that Perez did not come the first or second time when the Vidame [of Chartres] had audience, and that when he did, he came privately, and kissed the Queen's hand, but had no great speech with her; and that he has had two private conferences with her since. He never came publicly to Court, when the French ambassadors attended, except at the feast of St. George, and is unwilling to speak with many here, and the Queen unwilling to hear him; he has only spoken to the Lord Treasurer once, and then privately, and to the Earl of Essex once or twice; both have received great satisfaction in him, and much commend his sufficiency. It is not yet known whether he will stay here or return to France; nobody else is likely to deal with him; the Treasurer only desires to compare his judgment with his own experience, but the Earl seeks to get somewhat out of him upon which he may found some foreign action, for all his plots are to make the war offensive, rather than be driven to make it defensive.[6]

Francis Bacon, like his brother Anthony, was homosexual and was completely taken by the man to the point his mother wrote to Anthony of her fears for this relationship:

Though I pity your brother, yet so long as he pities not himself, but keepeth that bloody Perez, yea, as a coach-companion and bed-companion, a proud, profane, costly fellow, whose being about him I verily fear the Lord God doth mislike, and doth less bless your brother in credit, and otherwise in his health, surely I am utterly discouraged, and make conscience farther to undo myself to maintain such wrethces as he is, that never loved your brother but for his own credit, living upon him.[7]

Essex housed Perez in Gayness Park, Epping not far from Wanstead with an allowance of £20 a month, as well as being a valuable intelligence agent he was also a doctor specialising in bezoar stones – a remedy for poison – which Essex's sister Penelope swore by. His remedies were used by the earl's circle of friends but one prepared for Thomas Smith, one of Essex's secretaries, nearly killed him.

As the earl's intelligence network expanded, other connections would be made with agents in Florence, Venice, France, Spain,

Germany, Poland and even Transylvania. Essex's spy network was growing and along with it his importance to the queen. But it was not without its problems. Essex was angry with Phelippes for not delivering on a certain undisclosed mission which involved one Roger Walton who had yet to undertake his duties. Essex wrote to Phelippes that he heard Walton had not gone and 'this matter is nott to be playd withal, therefore I pray yow waken him, for besides the duty which wee all owe, my reputation is inganged in yt and I will not indure that the negligence of such a fellow shold turne to her Majestie's unquiettnes and my disgrace'.[8] But we do not know what disgrace Essex feared.

In May 1593 the poet and playwright, Christopher Marlowe, famous for his plays *Tamburlaine the Great* and later *Doctor Faustus* was stabbed to death at a house in Deptford owned by the widow Eleanor Bull. He had spent the day with Robert Poley, Nicholas Skeres and Ingram Frizer, all men of shady dealings. The coroner's report found that Marlowe had been stabbed above the right eye by Ingram Frizer in self-defence and he would be later pardoned for the poet's death. However rumours abounded at the circumstances of his death.

Later historians have found something fishy about the report and the fact that Frizer got off so easily. What were they all doing together? Marlowe also had dealings with the underground intelligence network and Nicholas Skeres had once worked for the Earl of Essex. Amongst many theories surrounding Marlowe's death is that Essex was using these men to force Marlowe to bring Raleigh down and their argument resulted in his death.

Essex certainly was expanding his intelligence network and probably employed men of a dubious nature but Skeres was no longer in his favour as a letter to Gelly Meyrick found in the Devereux papers proves.

Sir, it is long since I made choice of your friendship, and that

I have found you no more readier to do me good, hath (I think) rather proceded of my own negligence than your fault. Of which negligences I have in the wrong done to myself paid the price. But now I return to my self that have been long a stranger to my self, and do lay upon the love it hath pleased you to bear me, with this request to avoke your thoughts to help me in my present suit to my Lord [of Essex] which is for some employment and charge in these affairs that are now in hand which suit (being the only stay of my fortune and the readiest means for me to recover my umbered blemish) I present to you in his Lordship's favour to make me happy, and I shall be ready to do any service to the authors of my benefit. And though I have heretofore forsaken the ways of my good, I am so tired with those walks, as all my labour shall be spent to redress my life. Good Mr Meyrick respect my long service and travail the which I hope will not be so cast off and be now as ready to pleasure me as you have been willing before to show desire. I hope of your good will, I doubt not of your power, vowing if in this you make me happy to acknowledge you the only original and means of my good during life. Thus bending all my good in your goodness towards me, I wish you the happiness of your desires.[9]

That summer was hot and dry, feeding the plague and other illnesses but Essex continued to receive reports through Bacon, to attend the queen and welcome foreign dignitaries with lavish entertainments to the point that Elizabeth gave him £4000 to help towards his debts.

Elizabeth was in a foul mood in July when she heard Henri IV had become a Catholic. After all their campaigning and some success in the field, the French king had not been able to take control of Paris. On 25 July 1593, he formally renounced Protestantism and was reported to have said 'Paris is well worth a mass'.[10] Elizabeth had known he could not be trusted and she was appalled that now he was even closer to the enemy. The threat from Spain was still hanging over England and the queen was in a foul mood. It was not a good time to ask her for any favours but Essex was lobbying for Francis Bacon to become Attorney-General, a position vacated by Sir Thomas Egerton, who had moved on to become Master of the Rolls. Elizabeth however favoured Sir Edward Coke and Essex had a battle on his hands for Francis' preferment.

On 18 July Anthony Bacon wrote to his mother:

Our most honourable and kind friend the Earl of Essex was here yesterday three hours, and hath most friendly and freely promised to set up, as they say, his whole rest of favour and credit for my brother's preferment before Mr Coke's... His Lordship told me likewise he had already moved the Queen for my brother, and that she took no exceptions to him, but said that she must first dispatch the French and Scotch ambassadors and her business abroad, before she thinks of such home matters.[11]

Essex should have seen Elizabeth was just stalling. He wrote to Francis: 'I spake with the Queen yesterday and on Wednesday. On Wednesday she cut me off short; she being come newly home and making haste to her supper. Yesterday I had a full audience, but with little better success than before...'[12]

The queen was actually still angry with Francis' parliament speech and had no intention of giving the post to the man who had thwarted her in front of parliament but Essex persisted:

I told her that I sought for you was not so much your good, though it were a thing I would seek extremely and please myself in obtaining, as for her honour, that those excellent translations of hers might be known to them who could best judge of them. Besides, my desire was that you should neither be stranger to her person nor to her service; the one for your own satisfaction, the other for her Majesty's own sake, who if she did not employ you should lose the use of the ablest gentleman to do her service of any of your quality whatsoever. Her humour is yet to delay.[13]

Elizabeth wanted Coke for the position of Attorney-General and losing patience with her favourite she made it plain where she stood. In October Essex had an unhappy letter to write to Anthony Bacon:

I have broken promise by necessity and not for negligence. I spake largely with the Queen on Saturday in the evening, and forced myself to get up this morning because the Queen on Saturday told me she would resolve this today. But ere I could get from the Queen to my chamber, pain so possessed my head and stomach, as I was sent to my bed, where I have remained ever since.

On Saturday the Queen kindly accepted your promise to come to her, and as she said herself, sorrowed for your sickness which arrested you on the way. She used many words which showed her opinion of your worth and desire to know you better. She was content to hear me plead for your brother, but condemned my judgement in thinking him fittest to be Attorney whom his own uncle did name but to a second place; and said that the sole exception against Mr Coke was stronger against your brother, which was youth... Today I found her stiff in her opinion that she would have her own way. Whereupon I grew more earnest than ever I did before, insomuch as she told me that she would be advised by those that had more judgement in these things than myself. I replied so she might be, and yet it would be more for her service to hear me than to hear them; for my speech had truth and zeal to her without private ends.[14]

He ends by telling Bacon 'Burn this'.

This may have been the first time Francis Bacon tried to leave Essex's employ. He approached his relatives, the Cecils, to see if they could do anything for him. It was Burghley however that had been adamant that Coke should receive the post and Robert, his son, told Francis in no uncertain terms to stick with the earl.

Whilst Anthony would always be loyal, Francis would not.

In October Essex was sent to Dover with Lord Admiral Howard to supervise the defence of Ostend and check defences along the south coast and the Isle of Wight. He did his job but his mind was on far greater and more sinister things. He knew his relationship with Elizabeth was fractious and as in the case of Bacon's preferment, she did not always give him all he desired but he wanted to prove himself to her and make her realise she could not be without him. He thought that if he showed his worth, more favours would follow and he saw a way of doing that through his spies and their information.

The queen's physician Dr Lopez, a Portuguese Jew, had arrived in England back in 1558. He had studied anatomy at the University of Coimbra but was forced to leave his homeland due to the Spanish Inquisition. He soon found work at St Bartholomew's hospital in Smithfield and by 1571 had treated Lord Burghley and also ministered to Walsingham and Leicester before becoming the queen's physician on a salary of £50 a year.

But Lopez was also well connected through family and trade to Portuguese intelligence and provided information to Lord Burghley and possibly Walsingham before him. By the time he came under Essex's scrutiny, he had been working for many years as part of the Elizabethan spy network.

Lopez had once been close to Don Antonio de Crato, the deposed King of Portugal, but their relationship had deteriorated and the doctor brought a suit against him before the Privy Council on 21 December 1589 to recoup the losses he had suffered during his service. His hatred of Antonio led him to conspire with Manuel d'Andrada, a spy for King Philip II of Spain to assassinate Don Antonio with the aim of putting Don Emanuel on the throne. Andrada met with Philip II and received a ruby ring to give to Lopez as part-payment for his services. But Andrada was also working for Lord Burghley.

Essex was Don Antonio's patron but at this point he knew

nothing of the plot to kill him. He had in fact asked Lopez to also work for him prompting the doctor to ask the queen for permission. Lopez was walking a fine line between working for the two main intelligence networks in England plus being involved in his own sub-plots.

But Essex began to mistrust the man. He knew that when he gave news to the queen it was old. Lopez had already told Burghley and the queen had already been informed making him a laughing stock. Essex also began to suspect the doctor was spying on him and reporting back to Burghley.

Lopez had much to hide. He had linked up with Emanuel Luis Tinoco who worked for the Count of Fuentes, leader of the Spanish army in the Netherlands, whom Andrada also reported to. Tinoco was a many talented intelligencer who worked between camps selling information to some, keeping other secrets back ready to be used. The Count of Fuentes wanted Antonio Perez killed and Lopez agreed to be involved.

But Lopez also sensed that Essex was beginning to suspect him and look deeper into his negotiations. In an effort to create problems for the earl and jeopardise his status, Lopez visited Antonio Perez and Don Antonio at his monastery in Eton and told them 'some secrecies'[15] of Essex's medical history to shame him and bring about his fall. Although we don't know exactly what was said it is believed he referred to having treated him for syphilis – a rampant disease that was a taboo subject in Elizabethan times. Why Lopez chose these two to spread his rumour is hard to imagine – they were both beholden to the earl and immediately told him. If Essex had not disliked the doctor before now he was positively against him and determined to bring him down.

Around this time Anthony Bacon found out that one Esteban Ferreira da Gama was spying for Spain and might be linked to Lopez. On Thursday 18 October 1593 Essex had Ferreira arrested and given to Don Antonio for questioning. Instructions were sent to Rye, Sandwich and Dover to intercept any incoming Portuguese correspondence and this netted Gomez d'Avila who had arrived with letters for Ferreira.

Ferreira was interrogated and admitted that Dr Lopez had been spying for the Spaniards. But Essex did not rush to the queen with his confession. He wanted to find out more, convinced that this conspiracy could lead back to the Cecils and give him a chance to bring them down. He did however tell her 'how far doctor lopez was touched'[16] but Elizabeth knew her doctor worked for Burghley and only saw this suggestion as Essex making trouble. Instead she wanted Ferreira's papers re-examined by someone who could translate Portuguese well and for this she chose Lopez. Happy with his work she let the matter drop but Essex could not.

While the earl schemed to find out more the doctor, Lopez took the chance to complain to the queen of Essex's behaviour but he went too far and also suggested she should trick King Philip into paying 50,000 crowns promised to him originally for services rendered under Don Antonio but now held by the Spanish. 'Such was his impudency, to propound to Her Majesty what a good deed it were to cosen the King of Spain. Which speech uttered by him purposely, Her Majesty in her princely disposition did both greatly mislike, and sharpely reprehend'[17] the doctor.

Essex was in a quandary. Things were not moving fast enough and he was despairing of his relationship with the Cecils and the fiasco over Francis Bacon's application for Attorney-General. He went missing from court for three days. Two weeks later he was absent again for four days and the queen was on the point of sending out a search party when he returned. Yet all was well at the Twelfth Night celebrations when the queen was seen sitting on her throne by Anthony Standen, the returned spy, and 'was so beautiful to my old sight as ever I saw her' with Essex by her side 'whom she often devised in sweet and favourable manner'.[18]

When Don Antonio left England that year he sent a letter to the queen denouncing Lopez as a traitor but Essex still did not have enough proof against him. Tinoco, currently in Calais, now wrote to Burghley in the New Year asking for permission to come to England claiming he had secrets to reveal. Once he arrived he was arrested and letters were found on his person containing incriminating evidence. Essex and Robert Cecil were given permission to interrogate Tinoco but he 'held his mouth so close, and had his teeth so well conned, as a man might easier pluck out his teeth than the truth'.[19]

Essex tried another tack and this time showed the queen Ferreira da Gama's confession. Faced with this evidence she ordered that Lopez should be questioned. Lopez denied everything and was taken to Essex House under the guard of Gelly Meyrick. He was shown Ferreira's confession and was eventually led to admit he had seen correspondence from Spain. It was the first time he had admitted any contact with the Spaniards and Essex thought this was enough to condemn him.

On 25 January he went to the queen with his findings but she was unimpressed. 'Rash and temarious youth, to enter into a matter against the poor man which you cannot prove, and whose innocence I know well enough!' she ranted at Essex leaving him reeling.[20] He sulked for two days before returning to the queen and in a dramatic flourish told her 'I do no doubt but that he played the villain on both sides, and did intend to poison the Queen!'[21] It was a statement that could not be ignored. Lopez was sent to the Tower.

Three days later Essex wrote to Anthony Bacon 'I have discovered a most dangerous and desperate treason. The point of the conspiracy was Her Majesty's death; the executioner should have been Dr. Lopez; the manner by poison. This I have so followed as I shall make it appear as clear as noon-day'.[22]

But as yet he still did not have any proof and his mention of poison had just been a dramatic flourish. Essex and Robert

Cecil were sent to interrogate Lopez. The physician vehemently protested his innocence but he slipped up. He was asked about a ruby ring supposedly given to him from Phillip II for his services. He told his accusers that it had been sold but although the search of his house had not revealed incriminating papers they had found the ring. This at least was proof that the doctor was lying.

Sharing a coach after Lopez's examination Robert Cecil would also stir the pot with Essex by suggesting that promoting Bacon for the lesser position of Solicitor-General might be easier for the Queen to digest to which the earl responded

> digest me no digestions, the Attorneyship for Francis is that I must have; and in that I will spend all my power, might, authority and amity, and with tooth and nail defend and procure the same for him against whomsoever: and whosoever getteth this office out of my hands for any other, before he have it, it shall cost him the coming by.[23]

Robert in fact was just needling Essex because of his insecurity. He had worked out Lopez's greatest secret was wanting to kill Don Antonio Perez. It compromised the Cecils, implicating them in the plot and linked them to Tinoco. Lopez had been their Spanish agent and they had protected him but now he was endangering them all. On 8 February William Wade, clerk of the Privy Council, took over the investigation. He was very much in Burghley's pocket and would make sure that no confessions implicated the Cecils.

Ferreira da Gama was re-examined and this time coached by Wade he admitted 'the doctor said, if he might have 50,000 crowns given him, he was content, and would poison the Queen of England'.[24] Tinoco made a similar confession and then it was Lopez's turn. He was told of the other confessions and then he too said 'I never meant to do it, but Ferreira meant verily her

Majesty should have been destroyed with poison. I told Ferreira that I would minster the poison in a syrup. Which I said because I knew her Majesty never doth use to take any syrup'.[25] Lopez hoped that the queen would see from this he was telling the truth and had never conspired to murder her. He may have had secrets to hide but he had not conspired to kill the queen.

It was enough to send him to trial on 28 February. Lopez pleaded not guilty to the charge delivered by Sir Edward Coke that he 'did conspire, imagine and fantasise the death and destruction of the Queen's Majesty, and to stir Rebellion and War within the Realm, and to overthrow that State of whole common weal of this Realm'.[26] After the case for his prosecution was put forward he said of his confession 'I lied only to save myself from racking'.[27] Given he was in his seventies, there was definitely an element of truth to his statement. He was found guilty and sent back to the Tower but there he stayed for three months.

The queen had not interceded to stop the progress of the trial. The law had to be obeyed but she did not want her doctor's death on her conscience. When he wrote to her from the Tower she sent noncommitting replies and at court refused to sign his death warrant. Not until the death of Lord Strange in April did Elizabeth begin to reconsider. The lord had spent 16 days vomiting blood amidst rumours of poison. The scare was enough to make her rethink. Still she put nothing in writing but only verbally agreed to the death sentence being carried out.

On 7 June Lopez, Tinoco and Ferreira were taken before Chief Justice, Sir John Popham. Edward Coke was now ensconced as Attorney-General, the position that Bacon had so coveted and Essex had so wanted for him. He read out the charges against the defendants and allowed them to respond. Lopez reiterated 'I never thought to harm her Majesty'.[28] There was to be no reprieve. Popham issued a writ for their execution and from there they were led to Tyburn, hanged, drawn and quartered.

Elizabeth made no comment but she attached Lopez's ruby

ring to her waist and wore it for the rest of her life. Essex may have uncovered a plot but it was no victory. He would get no thanks from the queen.

Elizabeth did however give her approval for his sister Dorothy's next marriage. Thomas Perrot had died and in 1594 Dorothy married Henry Percy, the 9th Earl of Northumberland known as the 'wizard earl' for his love of science and alchemy. Their relationship would be a fractious one and Essex would often counsel his sister especially on how to correspond with her husband suggesting 'you have written to him letters of contrary styles, some that heal, and others again that rankle the wound you have made in his heart, which makes him think you unconstant and commanded by your passions'.[29] He may as well have been talking about himself.

Christopher Marlowe

Chapter Six

A Voyage to Cadiz

1595–1596

Essex was a mentor and patron for several young men who travelled abroad. He encouraged their sojourns not only to improve their outlook but to nurture new potential correspondents. One such young man was Roger Manners, the 5th Earl of Rutland, to whom he wrote a long letter including this advice.

> *Your Lordship's purpose is to travel, and your study must be what use to make of your travel. The question is ordinary, and there is to it an ordinary answer, which is, that your Lordship shall see the beauty of many cities, and learn the language of many nations. Some of these things may serve for ornaments, and all of them for delights; but your Lordship must look further than these, for the greatest ornament is the inward beauty of the mind; and when you have known as great variety of delights as this world can afford, you will confess that the greatest delight is sentire se indies fieri meliorem; to feel that you do every day become more worthy; your Lordship's end and scope should be that which in moral philosophy we call cultura anima, the tilling and manuring of your own mind.*[1]

Whether the earl took his advice or not, he did become one of Essex's most loyal supporters and would marry his stepdaughter, Elizabeth Sidney.

The queen still found Essex's intelligence valuable, even after the Lopez debacle, and the earl was high in favour but as ever it wasn't long before his relationship with his sovereign soured. Writing his will in 1595 he acknowledged and left provision for

'Walter Devereux the base and reputed son of the said Robert Earl of Essex begotten of the body of Elizabeth Southwell'.[2] Elizabeth finally knew the truth and was furious with him. Not only had he hidden the truth from her for years but she had also blamed and imprisoned Thomas Vavasour for the deed. She had been made a fool of and she was not pleased.

Henry Wriothesley, Earl of Southampton, was encouraged to take Essex's place as favourite during their time of estrangement, but he was another young man who had become a firm supporter of the earl's pledging his service to him. Southampton had also been one of Burghley's wards before spending four years at Cambridge. He was a patron of the arts and two of Shakespeare's poems, 'Venus and Adonis' and 'The Rape of Lucrece', were dedicated to Southampton in 1593 and 1594 leading some to believe he was Shakespeare's patron or even that they were lovers. Whatever his relationship to the bard he was a faithful and loyal friend to Essex and refused to be pushed into taking his place in the queen's favours.

Another man Essex had grown closer to was Anthony Bacon and in 1595 he moved into Essex House. Anthony's mother was unimpressed with his move writing:

I beseech God his blessing may follow you and be upon you wherever you go. The counsel to part with that London house so well agreed and most necessary was more cunning than regret for your good, being gouty as you be, but you are in such things to your great hurt credulous, and suffer yourself willingly to be abused. For the other place, though honourably offered, shall find many inconveniences not light. Envy, emulation, continual and seasonal disquiet to increase your gout, great urging for suits, yea importune, to trouble the Earl as well as yourself. Peradventure not so well liked yourself there as in your own house... I fear, having as you have working about you, some increase of suspicion and disagreement, which may hurt you privately if not publicly, or both, by all likelihood these evil times. The Lord help, and I have not mentioned before your unavoidable cause of expense. The manner of your removal goes to my heart...[3]

Yet it was easier for Anthony, with his ailments and debilitating gout, to live and work at Essex House and Essex was still trying for preferment for his brother Francis. But Elizabeth decided to give the position of solicitor-general to Sergeant Thomas Fleming despite Essex trying to dissuade her. Essex was so enraged and shamed by the whole experience he rode out to Francis and told him:

The queen hath denied me yon place for you, and hath placed another; I know you are the least part of your own matter, but you fare ill because you have chosen me for your mean and dependence; you have spent your time and thoughts in my matters: I die if I do not somewhat towards your fortune: you shall not deny to accept a piece of land which I will bestow upon you.[4]

The land was Twickenham Park where Francis had been living. Once leased by Bacon's half-brother Edward, Essex ensured that Francis now held the lease even though he could do no more for him.

Essex was entering an unhappy stage in his life. Robert Parsons, a Jesuit in exile, published *A Conference about the Next Succession to the Crown of England* under the name of Doleman which named fourteen possible successors. The book was dedicated to Essex:

To the Right Right Honourable the Earl of Essex, one of Her Majesties Privy Council.

Two principal Causes among others, (Right Honourable,) are wont to invite men to dedicate any Book or Treatise to a Person in Authority; The one, Private Duty and Obligation, the other, Publick

Utility, in respect that the Master may concern that Person for the Common Good. And to confess the truth, both of these jointly have moved me at this time to present unto your Honour, above others, the two Books ensuing, which contain a Conference had in Holland not long since, out the Pretences and Pretenders to the Crown of England, as your Honour shall perceive by the Preface of each Book, and therefore hereof I shall need say no more, but only declare the aforesaid two Causes of this Dedication.

First then I say, that my particular obligation towards your Honours Person, riseth partly of good Turns and Benefits received by some Friends of mine at your Lordships hands, in your last Voyage and Exploits in France, but principally of far greater Favours receiv'd from your Noble Ancestors, I mean not only your Father whose untimely death was to England no small Wound, but of your Grand-father also, that worthy Knight, Sir Walter Deverux, who though he lived not to come to those Titles of Honour, whereunto he was born; yet left he behind him so rare a memory for his excellent Parts of Learning, Wit, Feature of Body, Courtesy, and other such Noble Commendations, as none in England perhaps the like in our time, wherein also hath lived your Honours Great Grandfather, Sir Henry Deverux Visconde Ferys well remembred yet by divers of my said Friends obliged unto him as also recorded by our English Histories, as well for his Merits and Worthiness, as in like manner for his Match with the Heir of the most Famous and Noble House of the

Bourchers Earls of Essex, whereof also your Honour is known to be descended, and to hold at this day, as well their Nobility of Blood, as Dignity of Title, and this shall serve in this place for my particular obligation, whereof perhaps hereafter upon other occasion I may give further relation and testimony to the World, in token of my Gratitude.

But for the second Point of Publick Utility, I thought no man more fit than your Honour to dedicate these two Books unto, which treat of the Succession to the Crown of England, for that no man is in more high and eminent Place or Dignity at this day in our Realm, than your self, whether we respect your Nobility, or Calling, or Favour with your Prince, or high Liking of the People, and consequently no man like to have a greater part or sway in deciding of this great Affair, (when time shall come for that determination,) then your Honour, and those that will assist you, and are likest to follow your Fame and Fortune:

And for that it is not convenient for your Honour to be unskilful in a matter which concerneth your Person and the whole Realm, so much as this doth, and finding this Conference had by two Learned Lawyers, to handle the Question very pithily and exactly, and yet with much Modesty, and without offence of any, and with particular affection and devotion to Her Majesty, and with special care of Her Safety: I thought not expedient to let it lie unpublished, as also judged that no Hands were fitter to receive the same, nor any Protection more secure or plausible, than that of your Honour, whom God long preserve in all true Honour and Felicity to the Comfort of Your Lordships Faithful Servants and Clients, and to the Publick Benefit of your Countrey: From my Chamber in Amsterdam this last of December. 1593.[5]

The book also suggested that on Elizabeth's demise he would 'have a greater part or sway in deciding of this great affair'.[6] It made Essex out to have far more influence than he actually had and the queen, touchy enough about succession issues and knowing of the earl's correspondence with James IV, king of Scotland, was even more infuriated at the implication that Essex would be instrumental in choosing her successor.

Essex took to his bed, sick with worry and as Leicester before him, he used illness to illicit the queen's sympathy. It worked and the queen even visited him at his sickbed and fed him broth. Illness and depression always descended when he was out of favour. Whether real or imagined it turned into a repetitive vicious cycle. Still accession day was drawing close and it was not to be missed. Essex 'put off the melancholy he fell into' to organise his part in the celebration.

For his role in the entertainments, Francis Bacon wrote *The Philautia Device* (or *Of Love and Self-Love*) and possibly *The Device of the Indian Prince* for Essex to perform before Elizabeth.

My Lord of Essex's device is much commended in these late triumphs. Some pretty while before he came in himself to the tilt, he sent his page with some speech to the queen, who returned with her Majesty's glove. And when he came himself, he was met with an old Hermit, a Secretary of State, a brave Soldier, and an Esquire. The first presented him with a book of meditations; the second with political discourses; the third with orations of brave-fought battles; the fourth was but his own follower, to whom the other three imparted much of their purpose before he came in. [They] devised with him, persuading him to this or that course of life, according to their inclinations. Comes into the tiltyard unthought upon the ordinary postboy of London, a ragged villain all bemired, upon a poor lean jade, galloping and blowing for life, and delivered the Secretary a packet of letters, which he presently offered my Lord of Essex; and with this dumb show our eyes were fed for that time.

The device continued in the afternoon.

In the after-supper, before the Queen, they first delivered a well-penned speech to move this worthy knight to leave his vain following of Love, and to betake him to heavenly meditation: the secretaries all tending to have him follow matters of state, the soldiers persuading him to the war; but the esquire answered them all, and concluded with an excellent but too plain English, that this knight would never forsake his mistress's love, whose Virtue made all his thoughts divine, whose Wisdom taught him all true policy, whose Beauty and Worth were at all times able to make him fit to command armies. He showed all the defects and imperfections of all their times, and therefore thought his course of life to be best in serving his mistress. The old man was he that in Cambridge played Giraldy, Morley played the Secretary, and he that played Pedantiq was the soldier, and Toby Matthew acted the Squire's part. The world makes many untrue constructions of these speeches, comparing the Hermit and the Secretary to two of the lords, and the Soldier to Sir Roger Williams; but the Queen said that if she had thought there had been so much said of her, she would not have been there that night, and so went to bed.[7]

The device included a sonnet Essex had penned, previously attributed to Francis Bacon.

Seated between the old world and the new
A land there is no other land may touch,
Where reigns a queen in peace and honour true;
Stories or fables do describe no such.
Never did Atlas such a burthen bear
As she in holding up the world oppressed,
Supplying with her virtue everywhere,
Weakness of friends, errors of servants best.
No nation breeds a warmer blood for war,
And yet she calms them with her majesty.
No age hath ever wit refined so far,
And yet she calms them by her policy.
To her thy son must make his sacrifice,
If he will have the morning of his eyes.[8]

Elizabeth was unimpressed. Essex had planned the device to underline his devotion to his queen and show off his military ardour as a reflection of his loyalty to her but many took it as a stab at the Cecils and Elizabeth rather than seeing his love portrayed for her saw only Essex's love for himself. She was suitably unimpressed with his self-promotion. After the pageant excerpts of the script were circulated and he had Nicholas Hilliard paint him in his tournament finery with the queen's favour – her glove – clearly visible. Elizabeth was not amused.

Essex had been pushing to return to France and was eager to see England at war with Spain. He had been at home far too long and was restless and anxious to prove himself again, seeking another chance to shine and another opportunity to please his queen. Henri IV was at war with Spain, even though he was now a Catholic, and still wanted England's support. The earl was chomping at the bit to take troops across the Channel but Elizabeth was reluctant. His last time in France had been a costly fiasco. She did not want a repeat performance just to assuage Essex's need for glory.

While Essex continued to press for military command, he was saddened at the loss of a man he thought of as one of the greatest military commanders, Sir Roger Williams. Williams, a fiery Welshman, had been knighted by Leicester at the Battle of Zutphen and was with Essex at the Siege of Rouen. He had advised Essex on military strategy and wrote *A Brief Discourse of War, with his opinions concerning some part of Martial Discipline.* He died at Baynard's Castle on 13 December leaving all his possessions to the earl. Essex saw that he was buried with full honours at St Paul's and acted as chief mourner.

But the losses did not end there. Lord Huntingdon, once his siblings' guardian, was fatally ill in York and Essex rode north to be with him. He died on 17 December and Essex stayed in York till early January 1596. Returning to court it was not long before news filtered in that In Sir John Hawkins and Sir Francis Drake had died fighting the Spanish near Puerto Rico. It seemed that dysentery had carried off both of the seafaring captains and within weeks of each other they were buried at sea.

News also came of Philip II's preparations for war and the Privy Council decided to send 12,000 men to assault Cadiz,

Spain's premier seaport, under the command of Essex, Walter Raleigh, the Lord Admiral and his brother Thomas Howard but amidst their own preparations intelligence arrived that Calais was under attack from Spanish forces. Not only that but they could hear the cannon shot in London. Again Elizabeth was loath to commit her men to aid a king who had cost her £350,000 and not paid her back a penny. She was convinced to send troops by her councillors but then she changed her mind. Henri IV would not agree to her terms which included leaving English men to garrison the port. By the time the queen agreed to send an assault party it was too late. Calais fell on 24 April.

The expedition to Cadiz was back on. Essex and the Lord Admiral arrived in Plymouth at the end of April to organise men and ships. But now Elizabeth was complaining of the delay. Essex wrote to Robert Cecil:

> *Here I have our full number and here I keep them without spending our sea victuals or asking allowance or means from her majesty. I am myself, I protest, engaged more than my state is worth... yet I am so far from receiving thanks as her Majesty keepeth the same form with me as she would do with him that through his fault or misfortune had lost her troops. I receive not one word of comfort or favour by letter, message, or any means whatsoever.*[9]

Not only had he not heard from the queen but when he did she was demanding his recall and that of the Lord Admiral. She might even cancel the expedition all together. Essex had had enough. She would not snatch this chance from him. They were almost ready to sail and he raged:

> *What shall be done with the £30,000 worth of victuals of her Majesty already provided, since it cannot be sold to London nor to the ports, they themselves having provided more than they can utter? What shall come of the preparations of the city and the coasters? And how*

it may be hoped for, that upon the like summons they will show the like readiness, since they shall see that our alarms are but false and our journeys but dreams?[10]

Elizabeth's councillors persuaded her to despatch orders for the fleet to sail which Essex received on 24 May along with a prayer composed by the queen to read out to the troops and one for him 'I make this humble bill of requests to Him that all makes and does, that with His benign hand He will shadow you so, as all harm may light beside you, and all that may be best hap to your share; that your return may make you better and me gladder'.[11]

The fleet of 120 ships sailed on 1 June but were beaten back by bad weather. After two days they were able to sail again and make for the coast of Spain. Once at sea Essex sent a letter to the Privy Council. Elizabeth had ordered they destroy the Spanish fleet and return with their plunder but Essex wanted to garrison the port of Cadiz with English soldiers against her instructions. While he awaited a response to his suggestion, the town had to be taken.

Essex tried to land troops on the west side of Cadiz but the waves were too high and two of the smaller boats carrying troops capsized drowning the 15 men on board who were weighed down with armour. Recalling the others back to their ships the command was given to attack by cannon shot aimed at the seventy of more Spanish ships in the port.

The gun battle raged for eight hours with Walter Raleigh sustaining a leg injury from flying splinters that would leave him with a limp for life. Essex was eager to storm the town and landed some three miles away with 1000 men. Approaching Cadiz they were met by 500 Spaniards who easily defeated fled back into the town shutting the gates. Breaches in the city wall meant Essex could lead the charge after them and by the next morning a white flag was seen flying from the castle. Cadiz was now in English hands.

Elizabeth had ordered that although the city should be looted its people should be spared. Essex held his soldiers to this as much as he could, forbidding the desecration of churches and allowing the safe passage of many to leave the city while his soldiers ransacked houses and homes for plunder. The biggest prize was sitting in the port aboard 36 merchant ships laden with cargo worth 12 million ducats. Essex tried to negotiate their ransom with the Duke of Medina Sidonia but during the night the Spanish set fire to the ships, a fire that would last three days and ensure that the English could never take their goods. This was the plunder Elizabeth had hankered for and Essex would be held responsible for its loss.

But for now the town was in his hands. He had not heard from the Privy Council and continued with his plan to garrison the port proclaiming himself Governor. He knighted 68 men including his faithful man Gelly Meyrick, another move that would infuriate the queen. Although he was eager to stay, the other captains urged him to set sail. It was suggested that perhaps they would encounter more merchant ships at sea and find the loot that the queen sought. He reluctantly agreed and Cadiz was destroyed before the English left its harbour.

On the return to England it was decided to raid the town of Faro. One more shot at the Spanish and a chance for plunder. But it was a depressing failure. Marching the troops ten miles inland gave the inhabitants of Faro warning of the fate that was about to befall them and they fled taking their possessions with them. Essex however raided the library of Bishop Jerome Osorius of many precious and rare books that would one day find their way to the Bodleian library.

Essex argued with the Lord Admiral who had decided to return home. Surely if they stayed at sea they could intercept more Spanish ships laden with treasure or what about a raid on Spanish-held Lisbon? His ideas were shot down and the earl desperate still to prove himself inwardly seethed as the ships sailed for England.

The Lord Admiral reached England on 8 August and Essex two days after. If the earl had wanted a rapturous welcome he was to be sorely mistaken. The queen was furious. The expedition had cost her £50,000 and with the soldiers taking most of the plunder she received very little return on her expenditure. Not only that but Essex had knighted many men – an act which she abhorred. Knighthoods were precious gifts which only she had the right to bestow to men of good families. Essex, she felt, dolled them out like sweets.

But the people had welcomed him back and London resounded with celebrations. This just further angered the queen who hearing of a sermon preached at St Paul's that had lauded her favourite, furiously curtailed any further festivities. She felt that for every heart he won, she lost one and was 'resolved to breake hym of his will'.[12]

Essex tried to disseminate his version of events in a paper *A True Relation of the Action at Cadiz the 21ˢᵗ June under the Earl of Essex and the Lord Admiral* but this the queen suppressed on pain of death. Her attitude was infuriating and Essex was enraged at the situation and even further annoyed that during his absence Robert Cecil had been made Principal Secretary. The aging Burghley had now seen his son placed in high esteem with the queen but to Essex it seemed that while he was away his enemies had been working against him.

Although when Elizabeth heard that he had wanted to delay their return home to capture more Spanish merchant ships and that they had only missed those ships by two days she forgave him. He had been right after all and looking to swell her coffers. Instead she now blamed the Lord Admiral, Raleigh and Vere for not listening to her beloved earl. Essex was back in favour and grew his beard 'Cadiz-style', setting a new fashion. Even Burghley spoke up for him when the queen suggested she take

Essex's per cent of the ransom of his prisoners which earned her loyal secretary such displeasure that he retired to his country seat of Theobalds. Burghley was aging, tired and worn out with years of service.

He wrote to Essex:

My hand is weak, my mind troubled... I came from the Court with the burden of Her Majesty's displeasure, expressed as my Lord Buckhurst and Mr Fortescue did hear with words of indignity, reproach, and rejecting of me as a miscreant and a coward, for that I would not assent to her opinion that your Lordship ought (not) to have the profit of the prisoners, wishing her to hear you, both with what conditions your Lordship received them ... but herewith Her Majesty increased her ireful speeches, that I, either for fear or favour, regarded you more than herself...[13]

He also felt that Essex was displeased with him. It is a touching letter that showed Burghley's exhaustion and Essex replied to assure him he was still 'most disposed to do your Lordship's service'.[14] For all their butting of heads, Essex respected the elderly statesman.

Francis Bacon meanwhile was becoming more concerned with his master's relationship with the queen. He set down his thoughts and advice in a letter dated 4 October. He told Essex that the queen was often displeased with him for four main reasons; he did not like to be ruled, he was a soldier, he was too popular with the people and his estate was not equal to his ambition. Bacon asked him 'whether there can be a more dangerous image than this represented to any monarch living, much more to a lady, and of her Majesty's apprehension?'[15] and he urged him to win the queen over before setting down in detail what he could do to change these impressions of him. On the first point he had this to say:

For the removing the impression of your nature to be opiniastre and not rulable; first and above all things I wish, that all matters past, which cannot be revoked, your lordship would turn altogether upon insatisfaction, and not upon your nature or proper disposition. This string you cannot upon every apt occasion harp upon too much. Next, whereas I have noted you to fly and avoid, in some respect justly, the resemblance or imitation of my lord of Leicester and my lord Chancellor Hatton; yet I am persuaded howsoever I wish your lordship as distant as you are from them in points of favour, integrity, magnanimity, and merit, that it will do you much good between the queen and you, to alledge them, as oft as you find occasion, for authors and patterns: for I do not know a readier mean to make her majesty think you are in your right way. Thirdly, when at any time your lordship upon occasion happen in speeches to do her majesty right, for there is no such matter as flattery amongst you all, I fear you handle it magis in speciem adornatis verbis, quam ut sentire videaris. So that a man may read formality in your countenance; whereas your lordship should do it familiarly, et oratione fida. Fourthly, your lordship should never be without some particulars afoot, which you should seem to pursue with earnestness and affection; and then let them fall, upon taking knowledge of her majesty's opposition and dislike. Of which, the weightiest sort may be, if your lordship offer to labour, in the behalf of some that you favour, for some of the places now void; choosing such a subject as you think her majesty is like to oppose unto: and if you will say that this is conjunctum cum aliena injuria, I will not answer, Haec non aliter constabunt; but I say, commendation from so good a mouth doth not hurt a man, though you prevail not. A less weighty sort of particulars may be the pretence of some journeys, which at her majesty's request your lordship might relinquish: as if you would pretend a journey to see your living and estate towards Wales, or the like: for as for great foreign journeys of employment and service, it standeth not with your gravity to play or stratagem with them. And the lightest sort of particulars, which yet are not to be neglected, are in your habits, apparel, wearings, gestures, and the like.[16]

What Essex thought of this advice, the pointing out of his faults and the ways in which to cure them, is not known. Did he see it as a personal attack or as well meaning? Did he even have time to ponder it as news came in of King Philip's fleet setting sail for England, a second armada, to revenge Cadiz and the real fear of another invasion gripped the court?

Francis Bacon had pointed out that his soldierly ways annoyed the queen but she needed them now. Whereas the Cecils favoured diplomacy, Essex wanted action. The second armada of 126 ships carrying 15,000 soldiers was making its way to land either in Ireland or Wales. Essex headed a special Council of War to prepare for the arrival of the Spanish but come December they heard that a storm had decimated the fleet in the Bay of Biscay and surviving ships had limped back to their ports.

But Essex was also to receive advice from another member of the Bacon family – Lady Bacon. Rumours had abounded that the earl was having an affair with a married woman possibly Elizabeth Stanley, Countess of Derby and Burghley's granddaughter. She had once been a potential bride for his friend Southampton but the earl had refused the match. Essex was associated with her in 1596 and the following year. Lady Bacon had heard the rumours and admonished him for 'your dishonourable, and dangerous to yourself, coursetaking, to the infaming a nobleman's wife, and so near about Her Majesty…'.[17]

Essex replied:

I protest, that this charge, which is newly laid upon me, is false and unjust; and that since my departure from England towards Spain, I have been free from taxation of incontinency with any woman that lives. I never saw or spoke with the lady you mean but in public places.[18]

Not much is known of his relationship with Frances, his wife, at this time and if his comment about 'any women that lives' is anything to go by, he hadn't been spending much time with her either.

Robert Devereux, 2nd Earl of Essex

Chapter Seven

To the Azores

1597–1598

In March 1597 Lord Cobham, Lord Chancellor and Warden of the Cinque Ports, died and Essex put forward his friend Robert Sidney for the position of warden. As before the queen had decided to give the role to someone else, this time Cobham's son, Henry. Essex was fed up and planned a trip to Wales to escape from court and his tumultuous relationship with the queen but a messenger interrupted his preparations with news that Elizabeth wanted to speak with him. Returning to court, much to his delight the queen offered him the position of Master of Ordinance, in charge of munitions.

Following on the scare of invasion that had gripped the country before the New Year, Essex planned an expedition to the Azores, islands through which treasure ships sailed, as another strike against the Spanish. In April the Cecils and Raleigh were invited to dinner at Essex House – the earl needed their support and Raleigh wanted Essex's help to convince the queen to restore him to his former position of captain of the guard. Raleigh was back after five years of disgrace and Essex was ready to support him 'his mind being full, and only carried away with the business he hath in his head of conquering and overcoming the enemy'.[1]

In amongst his preparations for the voyage ahead, Essex however had time for play and contrary to his assurances to Lady Bacon this involved one Elizabeth Brydges, daughter of Baron Chandos. Rumour had it that he was 'again fallen in love with his fairest B; it cannot choose but come to the Queen's ears, and then he is undone and all that depend on his favour'.[2] The queen did not know of their affair but she surely suspected it when Elizabeth and her friend, both maids of honour, went to watch the earl playing 'ballon' without permission. They were banned from court for three days.

In May the queen thought to cancel Essex's voyage but was convinced to let it go ahead. She sent him her best wishes, a watch, a 'fayre angel'[3] and a thorn as tokens. As well as raiding treasure ships that were on their way from Peru to Madrid he was to stop at Ferrol on the west coast of Spain and see whether the rumours of a new armada being readied were true. If so he was to destroy the fleet and stop their sailing. Essex had sole command but his other captains made up a Council of War. These five men were Lord Thomas Howard as vice-admiral, Raleigh as rear-admiral, Charles Blount, lieutenant of land troops with his second Sir Francis Vere and Sir Anthony Shirley as sergeant-major.

In June Essex put to sea heading for Plymouth to reconnoitre with other ships and to pick up troops but such a storm blew up it took them two weeks. Sailing again on the 10th high winds and lashing rain again drove the ships back to the English coast. Essex found himself at Falmouth and frustratingly had to make his way back to Plymouth. Raleigh had been successful in regaining his role as captain of the guard but now his ship had been damaged and more repairs were needed before the fleet could sail again.

On 23 July Essex received a letter from the Lord Admiral and the Cecils at Plymouth:

On the first return of her Majesty's ships, there was great uneasiness about your safety. Since the news most welcome to her Majesty and all of your arrival, she has considered whether you could in good time reunite the army, separated in so many places, and the ships impaired by storms. She understands by your letters that your resolution, derived from a noble mind, is to pursue your voyage...[4]

It was not until 17 August that they were ready to sail again but a third storm split the fleet and as Essex neared Ferrol he knew he could not launch any attack without his full quota of manned ships. The queen was informed and although unhappy this part of the expedition could not be carried out, she knew it was understandable.

One of the ships that had been scattered was Raleigh's and Essex was increasingly anxious and annoyed as to where he was. They eventually met up on 14 September and although it was an amicable meeting, it foreshadowed deterioration in their relationship. Essex had heard that the Spanish fleet were indeed in Ferrol but instead of turning back he went ahead with plundering the islands whilst waiting for a treasure fleet to turn up.

At Fayal, Raleigh went ashore first without orders robbing Essex of any glory. Essex was furious and seriously listened to calls for him to be hung for mutiny. But Raleigh had waited for the earl until his men, seeing the islanders fleeing with their possessions, grew mutinous. He had decided to land and head for the town although they found it empty. Waiting for Essex had cost them and as Essex was really to blame, he forgave Raleigh.

The fleet continued on to Graciosa then on to St Michaels where they heard treasure ships were approaching. They had sailed in the wrong direction and hastily had to turn their ships around. The delay cost them, for the captains had been warned the English were lying in wait. The Spanish had had time to weigh anchor in the port of Terceira and were now guarded by a fortress. After a sea chase the English captured just three smaller ships that had been cut off from the main fleet. They contained some cargo but Essex had missed the main prize.

What to do now? Essex called a Council of War which decided to take St Michaels via the town of Villa Franca. Landing their troops they found the town abandoned but stayed there living off the supplies and victuals they found in the houses while the rest of the fleet remained out at sea waiting for the order to march across the island. Raleigh rode the waves waiting for an order to land which never came. When a 1800-ton galleon laden with goods approached he gave chase firing shot after shot but before his men could board the ship, which was now on fire, it sunk taking its cargo with it.

Essex knighted more men but the expedition was a disaster. Setting out for the homeward journey on 8 October a storm blew up and scattered them all. Essex lost communication and command as each vessel made its own way back to England.

He arrived back in Plymouth on 26 October amidst sightings of Spanish ships near Falmouth. King Philip had taken the opportunity in their absence to sail another armada of 136 ships towards England. Essex wrote to the queen he would immediately put back out to sea but the queen refused to let him sail off again 'whereby our own kingdom may lie open to serious dangers'.[5] Luckily a storm scattered the Spanish ships forcing them to return.

Essex was back at court on 5 November to answer for the expedition that had not carried out its two major objectives. The queen was tired. Tired of her favourite who did not deliver on his grandiose schemes, tired of sinking money into his exploits, tired of his ineffectualness – and she showed it. Essex tried to justify himself as he always did but Elizabeth wasn't listening.

He also received a letter from the queen sent while he was at sea. It underlined how displeased she was: 'When we do look back to the beginning of this action which hath stirred so great expectation in the world and charged us so deeply, we cannot but be sorry to foresee already how near all our expectations and your great hopes are to a fruitless conclusion'.[6]

While he sulked he heard that the queen had raised Charles Howard, Lord Admiral, to become Earl of Nottingham in recognition of his role in the Cadiz expedition which stung the earl immeasurably. Howard was also to act as Lord Steward for the forthcoming parliament giving him precedence over Essex meaning he would have to walk behind him. Essex was so infuriated by this calculated slight that he withdrew to Wanstead.

Essex stayed away from Court and Parliament, pretending once more to be ill, wrapped up in his misery and depression. It may have been then he wrote his poem 'Change Thy Mind':

Change thy mind since she doth change,
Let not fancy still abuse thee.
Thy untruth cannot seem strange
When her falsehood doth excuse thee.
Love is dead and thou art free;
She doth live, but dead to thee.

Whilst she lov'd thee best awhile,
See how she hath still delay'd thee,
Using shows for to beguile
Those vain hopes that have deceiv'd thee.
Now, thou see'st although too late
Love loves truth, which women hate.

Love no more since she is gone;
She is gone and loves another.
Being once deceiv'd by one,
Leave her love, but love none other.
She was false, bid her adieu;
She was best, but yet; untrue.

Love, farewell, more dear to me
Than my life which thou preservest.
Life, all joys are gone from thee,
Others have what thou deservest.
O my death doth spring from hence;
I must die for her offence.

Die, but yet before thou die,
Make her know what she hath gotten.
She in whom my hopes did lie
Now is chang'd, I quite forgotten.
She is chang'd, but changed base,
Baser in so vile a place.[7]

He was depressed and didn't even return for Elizabeth's accession day celebrations. His ability to sweeten her with 'all the arte I have'[8] had failed him. But his friends warned him to stay away too long gave his enemies every opportunity of maligning him. Reluctantly he returned to Essex House but still refused to attend council meetings.

Sir Francis Vere who had been ill since the Azores trip recovered his health in December and hurried to the queen to give her his account of the voyage. He justified Essex's actions and blamed others for the disastrous expedition. The queen softened and asked Essex to come to court. He did but nothing Elizabeth had to say could soothe him. The French ambassador de Maisse was waiting to deliver a peace proposal at a council meeting and the queen wanted Essex to hear it but he refused to attend.

De Maisse met with the queen several times and his account of these meetings gives us a snapshot of Elizabeth as she was then.

She kept the front of her dress open, and one could see the whole of her bosom, and passing low, and often she would open the front of this robe with her hands as if she was too hot. The collar of the robe was very high, and the lining of the inner part all adorned with little pendants of rubies and pearls, very many, but quite small. She also had a chain of rubies and pearls about her neck... As for her face, it is and appears to be very aged. It is long and thin, and her teeth are very yellow and unequal, compared with what they were formerly, so they say,... Many of them are missing, so that one cannot understand her easily when she speaks quickly. Her figure is fair and tall and graceful in whatever she does; so far as may be she keeps her dignity, yet humbly and graciously withal.[9]

This was the queen that Essex was annoyed with. He was beginning to see her as the aging woman that she was and remained indignant at the way she had treated him. Nottingham's rise had galled him so badly he swore he would fight him or any of his kin in a duel. He returned to Essex House still sulking and swearing he would never return to court until he was recalled and made Earl Marshal. That would give him precedence over Nottingham. Even when he got his wish he still wasn't entirely happy with the patent and wrote to Cecil:

I send you back this paper in which I have been bold to make a note or two, and especially have underlined some lines where I am praised for too innocent virtues, where they are active virtues and not negative that should draw on a Prince to bestow a marshal's office. Expedition in this is all, for now the Queen's times of signing and the shortness of time betwixt this and Christmas... The conclusion also is merely impertinent and may, I think, be well left out.[10]

Essex's relationship with Robert Cecil had improved of late and when Cecil was sent to France to negotiate with Henri IV Essex stood in as secretary. Whether Cecil was anxious what he would do in the role or was just feeling generous he persuaded the queen to allow the earl to purchase the cargo of cochineal and indigo seized in the Azores for £50,000 from which he would make a profit and also to give him a payment of £7000. Essex sorely needed the income as his debts were still unmanageably high at £30,000.

Happy to be back in favour, the earl sat in parliament in January and was able to take the precedence he so craved. For now his relationship with the queen was good but his friend Southampton had caused trouble at court. After the queen had gone to bed one night, Southampton, Raleigh and a Mr Parker had stayed up late in the presence chamber gambling. When Ambrose Willoughby, Squire of the Body, asked them to stop Raleigh had gone to bed but Southampton ignored him until he was threatened with the arrival of the guard. The next day Southampton struck the man and a brawl ensued with the earl losing some of his hair. Essex's friend was banned from court until Elizabeth relented, pointedly giving him leave to accompany Cecil to France and remain abroad for two years.

Essex was playing host to his mother who was staying at Essex House. Gelly Meyrick, by now his steward, organised a Valentine's Day meal for the family including Essex's sisters and wife. The earl was close to his mother but Lettice continually asked him to obtain an audience for her with the queen. Since Lettice had been banned from court for marrying Leicester she had not been allowed into the royal presence. Essex managed to get the queen to agree to a meeting but his mother waited at court in vain. The earl tried again and:

> Upon Shrove Monday, the Queen was persuaded to go to Mr Controller's at the Tilt End, there was my lady Leicester with a fair jewel of £300. A great dinner was prepared by my lady Chandos, the Queen's coach ready and all the world expecting her majesty's own coming; when upon a sudden she resolved not to go and so sent word.[11]

Lettice was furious at the snub and Essex tried again arranging their meeting for 2 March. This time the queen showed up, allowed the earl's mother to kiss her and primly returned her embrace. Lettice was delighted and felt with Essex's renewed favour at court she now too would rise but the queen had had enough. She would not allow this woman to return to court nor did she ever want to see her again. Essex would just have to accept defeat and learn not to meddle in the queen's personal relationships.

Cecil returned from France in April with the news that Henri IV had secretly been negotiating with the Spanish. Essex called for more action against them but his fellow councillors were tired of his lust for war. Lord Burghley wanted peace quoting from his psalm book that 'men of blood shall not live out half their days'.[12] The state could not afford more war and Essex was overreaching. Others had noticed too and one poem written at the time ran:

> This vizard-fac'd pole-head dissimulation,
> This paraqueet, this guide to reprobation,
> This squint-ey'd slave, which looks two ways at once,
> This fork'd Dilemma, oil of passions,
> Hath so beray'd the world with his foul mire
> That naked Truth may be suspect a liar.
> For when great Felix (Essex) passing through the street,
> Vaileth his cap to each one he doth meet,
> And when no broom-man that will pray for him,
> Shall have less truage than his bonnet's brim,
> Who would not think him perfect courtesy?
> Or the honeysuckle of humility?
> The devil he is as soon: he is the devil,
> Brightly accoustred to be-mist his evil:
> Like a swartrutter's hose his puff thoughts swell,
> With yeasty ambition: Signor Machiavel
> Taught him this mumming trick, with courtesy
> To entrench himself with popularity,
> And for a writhen face, and body's move,
> Be barracadoed in the people's love.[13]

In June 1598 Essex composed his 'Apologie' pamphlet – in the format of a letter to Anthony Bacon to 'those which fasly and maliciously taxe him to be the onely hinderer of the peace, and quiet of his countrey'.[14] In it he answered his detractors with justifications of his actions in Portugal, his time in France and Spain and his expedition to the Azores. It pointed the finger at his enemies and annoyed the Cecils with its innuendo.

Essex was not everyone's favourite but the queen indulged him until in July they had their most serious argument. The earl's father had once been Lord Deputy of Ireland and the position once again became vacant in 1597 after Lord Burgh's death. Rumours suggested poison had ended his life as had been said of Essex's father, Walter. Now it was imperative to fill the role and Essex put forward Sir George Carew. Carew was no friend of the earl's and it was obvious to the queen he was nominating a man he disliked. Elizabeth favoured Sir William Knollys, his uncle, and their exchange grew more and more heated until Essex in exasperation turned his back on his sovereign. Enraged by his slight Elizabeth boxed his ears and screamed insults at him. Whirling round Essex drew his sword swearing he would never have accepted such insults from her father let alone her. Nottingham stayed his hand and the earl stormed out of the room leaving the queen shocked and silent.

But she did not call for his arrest nor order him to the Tower. No one had ever treated her thus and she let him. Essex returned to Wanstead and steadfastly refused to apologise.

Lord Keeper Egerton urged him to curb his behaviour:

The beginning and long continuance of this so unseasonable discontentment you have seen and proved, by which you may aim at the end. If you hold still your course, which hitherto you find worse and worse, (and the longer you tread this path, the farther you are still out of the way) there is little hope or likelihood that the end will be better than the beginning. You are not so far gone but you may well return. The return is safe, but the progress dangerous and desperate in this course you hold. If you have enemies, you do that for them which they could never do for themselves; whilst you leave your friends open to shame and contempt, forsake yourself, overthrow your fortunes, and ruinate your honour and reputation, giving that comfort to our foreign foes, as greater they cannot have. For what can be more welcome and pleasing news to them than to hear that her Majesty and the Realm are so maimed of so worthy a member who hath so often and so valiantly quailed and daunted them?[15]

Egerton also urged Essex 'to conquer yourself'. But Essex found it difficult to contain or conquer himself. He wrote to the queen but his letter was in no way an apology:

When I think how I have preferred your beauty above all things, and received no pleasure in life but by the increase of your favour towards me, I wonder at myself what cause there could be to make me absent myself one day from you. But when I remember that your Majesty hath, by the intolerable wrong you have done both me and yourself, not only broken all laws of affection, but done against the honour of your sex, I think all places better than that where I am, and all dangers well undertaken, so I might retire myself from the memory of my false, inconstant, and beguiling pleasures. I am sorry to write thus much, for I cannot think your mind so dishonourable but that you punish yourself for it, how little soever you care for me. But I desire whatsoever falls out, that your Majesty should be without excuse, you knowing yourself to be the cause, and all the world wondering at the effect. I was never proud, till your Majesty sought to make me too base. And now since my destiny is no better, my despair shall be as my love was, without repentance. I will as a subject and an humble servant owe my life, my fortune, and all that is in me; but this place is not fit for me, for she which governs this world is weary of me and I of the world. I must commend my faith to be judged by Him who judgeth all hearts, since on earth I find no right. Wishing your Majesty all comfort and joys in the world, and no greater punishment for your wrongs to me, than to know the faith of him you have lost, and the baseness of those you shall keep.[16]

Elizabeth had more to concern her than Essex's tantrums. Lord Burghley had been ailing for some time. He was 77 and had served the queen faithfully for 40 years. She had gone to his bedside, spooning broth into the old man's mouth, willing him to recover but this time there would be no remedy. When Elizabeth heard news of his death she shut herself away to mourn in private.

Essex attended a council meeting but the queen refused to see him and he stormed off. The situation in Ireland was worsening. On 14 August Sir Henry Bagenal, general of the English army in Ireland, fought to relive troops stationed at Blackwater(town) in Armagh but was overcome by Hugh O'Neill, the Earl of Tyrone and his troops. At the end of the skirmish at Yellow Ford over 2000 English soldiers were dead including Bagenal himself.

Essex was back at court on 22 August but again the queen refused to see him. He returned home to hear of another death, his cousin, Henry Bourchier, who left him all his 'books of histories, of Latin, French, Italian and Spanish, and such other of antiquities as he shall please to accept of'.[17] Back at home he composed a letter to the queen:

Yet when the unhappy news came from yonder cursed country of Ireland, and that I apprehended how much your Majesty would be grieved to have your armies beaten and your kingdom like to be conquered by the son of a smith, duty was strong enough to rouse me out of my deadest melancholy; I posted up and first offered my attendance, and after my poor advice in writing, to your Majesty. But your Majesty rejected both me and my letter. The cause, as I hear, was that I refused to give counsel when I was last called to my Lord Keeper's. But if your Majesty had not already judged this cause, or that I might appeal from your indignation to your justice,

I then should think your Majesty, if you had once heard me, would
clear me from all undutifulness.[18]

But he was given no response. Essex may have returned to
Wanstead or stopped awhile at Essex House. He visited Queen's
College, Cambridge having been made Chancellor on 25 August.
Whitgift, a previous chancellor himself, was one of his supporters
'knowing the disposition of the Earle of Essex towards learning
and learned men I doe not think any man in England so fit for
that office, as he is'.[19]

He was back in London for Lord Burghley's funeral on the
29th at Westminster Abbey where

Five hundred mourners, whereof were many noblemen, and among
the rest the Earl of Essex, who (whether it were upon consideration
of the present occasion, or for his own disfavours) me thought,
carried the heaviest countenance of the company: presently, after
dinner, he retired to Wanstead, where, they say, he means to settle,
seeing he cannot be received at court, though he have relented much,
and sought by divers means to recover his hold; but the Queen says
he hath played long enough with her, and that she means to play
awhile upon him, and so stand as much upon her greatness as he
hath done upon stomach.[20]

Whilst Essex returned home, Burghley was buried at St Martin's
Church, Stamford next to the memorial to his parents.

Essex skirted with more disfavour when he allowed his
friend the Earl of Southampton, who returned briefly from exile
in Paris, to marry his pregnant sweetheart and Essex's cousin,
Elizabeth Vernon, at Essex House. Elizabeth was one of the
queen's maids of honour and he invited the new countess to
reside in his London home. Of course the queen was not pleased
and told Cecil to write to Southampton which he did in no
uncertain terms:

...her Majesty knoweth that you came over very lately, and returned again very contemptuously: that you have also married one of her Maids of Honour, without her privity, for which, with other circumstances informed against you, I find her grievously offended: and therefore it hath pleased her to command me in her name to charge you expressly (all excuses set apart) to repair hither to London, and from thence to advertise us your arrival, without coming to the Court, until her pleasure be known.[21]

Fearing the queen's displeasure Southampton would not return for some weeks missing the birth of his first child, a daughter they would name Penelope.

Essex was still not allowed back at court. After many of his arguments with the queen he often became ill, whether feigned or real and at the beginning of September he had a fever. Elizabeth sent her physician to him along with Sir Henry Killigrew, Sir Fulke Greville and Lord Henry Howard to convey her good wishes and inform him he was at last permitted to return. He quickly rallied and resumed his courtly duties.

His sister Dorothy was delighted for him writing 'I cannot but desire to know how the court air and humours agree with you. If both sort with your health and contentment, none shall be more glad than your most affectionate sister'.[22] However Essex immediately pressed for the office of master of wards left vacant by Burghley. Although he may have been allowed back into the queen's presence she was not about to reward him. He acted like a petulant child and as soon as he was back in favour he always asked for more.

At around the same time one Edward Squires, who worked at the queen's stables in Greenwich was arrested. He was charged with trying to poison the queen and Essex on two separate occasions. He had administered poison to the pommel on the queen's saddle which he hoped would transfer to her skin and kill her but it had no effect. To try and kill the earl Squires had embarked on the Azores trip and taken poison with him to rub on Essex's chair.

I did this of an evening a little before suppertime, when the Earl was at sea between Fayal and St Michael. The confection was so clammy that it would stick to the pommel of the chair, and I rubbed it on with parchment; and soon after, the Earl sat in the chair at supper time.[23]

Again it did not work. Squires confessed at his trial and on 13 November was hanged, drawn and quartered at Tyburn. Both the queen and Essex had had a lucky escape.

The Accession Day celebrations held four days after gave Essex the chance to show off in front of the queen. But even now he could not resist a dig at Raleigh who he had heard would be wearing feathers of orange with his retinue – Essex's colour. The earl made sure that he entered with far more men and far more feathers, reportedly 2000 of them. The queen was not impressed with Essex's 'glorious feather triumph'[24] and ended the celebrations early. She was growing increasingly weary of her favourite's pettiness.

Chapter Eight

Essex's Final Command

1599

A more pressing position that was still vacant and needed to be filled was that of Lord Deputy of Ireland. The queen favoured Lord Mountjoy but the earl protested that the role needed someone with more military experience. Essex protested so loud and hard that the queen decided to send him instead. Well aware of the troubles in Ireland and his own father's death there, this was a commission he did not welcome but he had forced himself into an impasse.

By January 1599 he was writing 'Into Ireland I go. The Queen hath irrevocably decreed it; the Council do passionately urge it; and I am tied in mine own reputation to use no tergiversation'.[1] There was much to prepare and the queen generously let him off £10,000 of debt to aid the expedition.

But many were concerned about Essex and his lust for war. John Hayward wrote a book *The First Part of the Life and Raigne of King Henrie the III* which came out in February 1599 that drew on Shakespeare's play *Richard II* about his deposition and murder by Bolingbroke. It was dedicated to Essex and many drew parallels between Essex and the king's murderer. Elizabeth wanted Hayward charged with treason but Francis Bacon who had been forgiven and now had the ear of the queen was fast becoming something of an adviser to her and suggested that the charge ought to be theft for the author had stolen many sentences from Tacitus. Hayward would spend the rest of Elizabeth's reign imprisoned.

On 25 March 1599 Essex was officially made Lieutenant and Governor-General of Ireland. The Earl of Southampton had returned in November and was sent to the Fleet prison but was soon released. Essex wanted him as his master of horse in Ireland but the queen refused. Neither would she allow Sir Christopher Blount, his stepfather and marshal of the army, to join the Council of Ireland. Essex said his goodbyes to his wife, sister Penelope and Southampton's wife who were staying at Chartley.

As Essex reluctantly travelled towards the coast and feeling ill again he wrote:

> I did only move her Majesty for her service to have given me one strong assistant, but it is not her will. What my body and mind will suffice to, I will by God's grace discharge with industry and faith. But neither can a rheumatic body promise itself that health in a moist, rotten country, not a sad mind vigour and quietness in a discomfortable voyage. But I sit down and cease my suit, now I know her Majesty's resolute pleasure. Only I must desire to be freed from all imputation, if the body of the army prove unwieldy, that is so ill furnished, or so unfurnished, of joints; or of any main in service, when I am sent out maimed beforehand.[2]

Essex arrived in Dublin in the second week of April then situated in the English pale – an area controlled by the crown but outside of the pale was a country that resisted English authority. It had been notoriously difficult to conquer but England persisted afraid it would be a landing base for the Spanish and a stepping-stone to invasion.

The day after he arrived Essex was formally sworn in as Lord Lieutenant and received the sword of state before asking for a report on the current situation. The Council of War informed him there were 17,997 rebels, 8922 of which were in Ulster. Essex had in his command the largest army ever assembled in Ireland of 16,000 foot and 1300 horse.

The north was governed by Hugh O'Neill, Earl of Tyrone and both the queen and Essex had believed that the main thrust of this expedition would be to attack the earl and subdue his rebels but the Council thought otherwise. It would be better to attack Ulster when weather conditions were more favourable and more supplies had arrived from England. Rebels were amassing in Leinster and it was decided to head south west. Essex informed the Privy Council and asked for reinforcements. The queen agreed to this new plan but no reinforcements would be sent as yet.

Early in May Essex set out with 3000 soldiers and 300 horse for Athy, south-west of Dublin. Although he was head of a large army it was split with 5000 men needed to defend the Pale, others to defend the communication and supply routes and yet others to garrison castles and defend borders.

At Athy he accepted the fealty of Thomas Butler, 10th Earl of Ormonde, Lord Cahir and Lord Mountgarret and the surrender of the castle. One hundred men were left to defend it. They pressed on to Maryborough where they revictualled the garrison, leaving a further 500 men behind, before continuing on to the Pass of the Plumes at Cashel in Co. Tipperary where they encountered rebel activity. A skirmish ensued but with few English losses they cleared the pass and made their way to lavish receptions further south at Kilkenny and Clonmel. A further 1100 men had been stationed in Carlow and Offaly reducing the army yet again.

From Kilkenny Essex wrote to the Privy Council:

This people against whom we fight hath able bodies, good use of the arms they carry, boldness enough to attempt, and quickness in apprehending any advantage they see offered them. Whereas our new and common sort of men have neither bodies, spirits, nor practice of arms, like the others. The advantage we have is more horse, which will command all champaigns; in our order, which these savages have not; and in the extraordinary courage and spirit of our men of quality. But, to meet with these our helps, the rebels fight in woods and bogs, where horse are utterly unserviceable; they use the advantage of lightness and swiftness in going off, when they find our order too strong for them to encounter; and, as for the last advantage, I protest to your Lordships it doth as much trouble me as help me. For my remembering how unequal a wager it is to adventure the lives of noblemen and gentlemen against rogues and naked beggars, makes me contain our best men than to use their courages against the rebels.[3]

His next objective was to take Cahir Castle. Lord Cahir had given his fealty to the earl but the castle was held by rebels. By 23 May the army stood at 2500 foot and 300 horse whilst they waited at Clonmel for the cannon needed to take the castle. In the coming days Essex split the army into three; the vanguard to lead the march to Cahir, the main army and the rearguard to protect and move the cannon. Due to a lack of horses the cannon would have to be hauled by man power and what with bad roads and inclement weather it was a tortuous march.

Essex overtook the vanguard who were to wait one mile short of castle and sent Lord Cahir and Sir Henry Danvers to talk to the rebels holding the castle and assess its defences. Lord Cahir had promised the castle would surrender but was insolently jeered by the rebels who refused to lay down their arms.

Essex called a Council of War on 25 May with the Earl of Ormond, Sir George Bingham, marshal of the camp, the master of ordinance, the lieutenant of the Queens County and Sergeant-Major Sir Olyver Lambert. Cahir Castle, one of the largest castles in Ireland, sat on a rocky island in the River Suir. They were facing wet fighting conditions and a river ready to burst its banks. Supplies were low and rebels were amassing around the area. The next day the army moved closer on the east side of the river sticking to old ditches and freshly dug trenches. The rearguard arrived with the cannon and a platform was built to situate it but it appeared the rebels were unconcerned and still freely moving in and out of the castle.

Essex ordered Captain Brett and Captain Chamberlain of the Guards to capture the orchard island south of the castle with 300 men. It was a success even though Essex thought 40 men could have easily have held off 4000 there however Captain Brett was injured and later died.

By 27 May they were in position and ready to start firing. The main cannon was loaded and fired but after the second shot its undercarriage broke. A cannonball got stuck in the culverin, the second cannon, but after it was cleared it repeatedly fired over 50 shots throughout the day. Lord Cahir and his wife were supposed to have cried at the devastation it caused.

The following day, the cannon was repaired and remounted and the culverin moved closer. The castle was bombarded with shot badly damaging its walls. Essex ordered his men to prepare for an assault but that night the rebels tried to escape. Many were killed, over 80 cut down in the river or drowned whilst others swam for it and escaped.

By the morning, Essex's troops entered the castle without any resistance. The cannon were rolled within its walls and the breaches repaired. The earl left a hundred men to garrison it whilst he moved on.

The troops moved on to Limerick arriving on 4 June for a few days' rest. Moving on they encountered more rebels but the army was running low on supplies and this would be their last fight before turning east back to Waterford and from there crossing the river at Passage to head for Wexford and then up the south coast back to Dublin.

Essex wrote a long letter to the queen but he was not happy. After detailing his expedition and the state of Ireland he railed against her for her lack of support and blamed those who had her ear at court:

Is it not known from England I receive nothing but discomforts and soul's wounds? Is it not spoken in the army, that your Majesty's favour is diverted from me, and that already you do bode ill both to me and it? Is it not believed by the rebels that those whom you favour most, do more hate me out of faction, than them out of duty and conscience? Is it not lamented of your Majesty's faithfullest subjects, both there and here, that a Cobham or a Ralegh – I will forbear others for their places' sakes – should have such credit and favour with your majesty when they wish the ill-success of your majesty's most important action, the decay of your greatest strength, and the destruction of your faithfullest servants?[4]

During their expedition Essex had sent Sir Henry Harrington into the Wicklow Mountains. Harrington's troops engaged with the enemy near the Ranelagh River but were so overwhelmed by their greater numbers that the English fled for their lives. Essex was furious with their cowardice and ordered a court martial. Sir Henry Harrington as a privy councillor could not be tried and so was jailed to await her Majesty's pleasure. Piers Walshe, lieutenant, was executed. The officers and captains were cashiered and jailed whilst the soldiers involved were condemned to death although Essex informed the council 'were by me most of them pardoned; and for example's sake, every tenth man only executed'[5] to boost morale after the executions, Essex knighted – against the queen's wishes again – 12 men on the 12th and three on the 13th.

Elizabeth was unhappy that the Earl of Tyrone had still not been dealt with and she saw Essex's last few months in Ireland as a waste of time. She wrote him a long letter on 19 July and with no satisfactory reply she wrote again on 30 July:

First, you know right well, when we yielded to this excessive charge it was laid upon no other foundation than that to which yourself did ever advise us as much as any, which was, to assail the Northern Traitor, and to plant garrisons in his country, it being ever your firm opinion, amongst others of our Council, to conclude that all was

done in other kind in Ireland, was but waste and consumption ...
for the present, therefore, we do hereby let you know, that the state
of things standing as they do, and all the circumstances weighed,
both of our honour and of the state of that kingdom, we must expect
at your hands, without delay, the passing into the North, for
accomplishment of those counsels which were resolved on at your
departure, to the intent that all these six months' charges prove not
fruitless, and all future attempts there as little successful...[6]

Before Essex had left England she had agreed he could utilise a
deputy and return to court if needed but now she rescinded that
order adding to her letter that

you do now in no wise take that liberty, nor adventure to leave
that State in any person's government ... after you have certified
to us to what form you have reduced things in the north, what
hath been the success, and whom you and the Council could wish
to leave with that charge behind, that being done, you shall with
all speed receive our warrant, without which we do charge you (as
you tender our pleasure) that you adventure not to come out of that
kingdom, by virtue of any former licence whatsoever.[7]

Essex had his orders but things were not going well for him in
Ireland. On 5 August Sir Conyers Clifford died in the Curlew
Mountains near Boyle whilst leading troops to lift the siege on
Sir Donogh O'Connor's castle. Essex called a Council of War on
21 August and although the council disagreed with Elizabeth's
order to head north and confront the Earl of Tyrone, he felt it
must be done. He wrote 'I am even now putting my foot into the
stirrup to go to the rendezvous at Navan; and do as much duty
will warrant me and God enable me'.[8]

Whilst Essex was in Ireland, he had written to his wife and
around this time he received one back from Frances who had
been ill and staying at Barn Elms:

I have had the good fortune to receive two letters from you. The first came when I was so sick that I could not speak with Mr. Darci which brought it, but the joy which I took in receiving news from you did deliver me out of a fever which held me 03 hours without any intermitting in great extremity, but now, I thank my God, am free from it, but so much weakened by it that I am not able to come off my bed. None that sees me now would believe I were with child, for I am less than I was two months ago. Your son Boben is better than ever he was. I fear I shall never receive so great comfort of my other little one unless I quickly mend. I will for this time take my leave, being not able to endure long writing, but by the next messenger I hope to write you word of my amendment.[9]

On 3 September Essex and his army reached Ardee in Louth and there they saw Tyrone's troops which vastly outnumbered them. Tyrone sent his man O'Hagan to parley but Essex refused and instead put on his own show of strength. Sending O'Hagan again it was agreed Essex would meet Tyrone at the ford of Bellaclynth. They spoke privately and then returned to their troops. Essex knew he could not be beaten and had agreed to peace. The next day a truce was drawn up to last six weeks and to be reviewed every six weeks thereafter.

Returning to Dublin Essex received a letter from Elizabeth refusing to accept this 'hollow peace' not knowing he had already done so:

It appeareth by your journal that you and the traitor spoke half an hour together without any body's hearing; wherein, though we that trust you with our kingdom are far from mistrusting you with a traitor, yet both for comeliness, example, and your own discharge, we marvel you would carry it no better.

She continued by saying 'to trust this traitor upon oath is to trust the devil upon his religion'.[10]

But it was too late. Essex had agreed. He had made Southampton his master of horse against the queen's wishes and knighted over 80 men. He knew he was in trouble and Southampton urged him to return to London with at least 1000 men at his back. Sir Christopher Blount managed to dissuade them from such a perilous action. The queen would be angry enough, to take an armed force into the city would only make matters worse. Still without the queen's permission Essex handed over the sword of state to Archbishop Loftus and Sir George Carew and on 24 September left Ireland's shores.

Reaching England Essex rode for Nonsuch at great speed. Timing was everything. He had to get to the queen and speak to her personally before she heard any other reports. He was nearly thwarted by Lord Grey whom they met on the road and refused to make way. But Grey must have taken his news to Cecil rather than the queen as when Essex arrived ten minutes later he was able to burst through the palace straight into Elizabeth's private bedchamber.

The queen was in a state of undress. She had no time to put on her makeup or wig and had no idea what was going on when the earl threw himself at her feet, hot and sweaty from riding, clearly agitated. Where were her guards? She was alone with a man who had been her favourite but now she had no clue of his intentions. Frightened but coolly in control, she calmed him and asked him to return in a while when they were both more composed. As he left he told the astonished courtiers 'he found a sweet calm at home'.[11] On the face of it he had but Elizabeth was furious once her fear abated.

It is definitely curious that Essex so easily entered her bedchamber. Raleigh's guards should have stopped him but they were nowhere to be seen. Some have seen his hand, if not Cecils, in setting up the earl, having the guards dismissed and engendering Essex's fall. For he was about to enter the final phase of his tumultuous life.

The queen allowed Essex to return and talk for an hour and she realised he was not there to harm her but to try and excuse himself. She let him talk and then took time to consider the situation before recalling him and now she questioned him with full force. He had done enough, seen her undressed and at her lowest state. Now she was truly queen, sure of herself and ready for battle. She would not listen to his excuses and finally dismissed him. He did not know it but he would never see her again.

Essex was questioned by members of the council and after the queen had read their report she ordered Essex be confined to his chamber. In was called in front of the council the next day to answer to six charges:

> That Essex had been contemptuously disobedient to Her Majesty's instructions in returning to England.
>
> That many of his letters from Ireland had been presumptuous.
>
> That he had departed in Ireland from the instructions given to him before he left England.
>
> That his flight from Ireland had been rash and irresponsible in view of the situation there.
>
> That he had been overbold in breaking into Her Majesty's bedchamber.
>
> And that he had created an inordinate and unjustified number of idle knights while he had been in Ireland.[12]

Essex stood before the council and answered the charges against him for over three hours before returning to his chamber. The councillors gave Elizabeth their report and she took Sunday to deliberate over it. On Monday Essex was informed he was to be removed to York House and placed under house arrest. Lord Keeper Egerton, who had once counselled Essex on the error of his ways was charged with his custody. He would be allowed no visitors and only two servants. Soon he plummeted into the depression that had always haunted him. He was ill again but the queen was no longer listening to his pleas nor succumbing to the allure of her favourite. For two months he remained in this state without any formal trial or decision over his future.

Raleigh was certainly no friend to the earl at this point and would later say that Essex had called the queen as crooked as her carcass. He saw trouble brewing and urged Robert Cecil to look to him:

Sir, — I am not wise enough to give you advice; but if you take it for a good counsel to relent towards this tyrant, you will repent when it shall be too late. His malice is fixed, and will not evaporate by any of your mild courses; for he will ascribe the alteration to her majesty's pusillanimity and not to your good nature, knowing that you work but upon her humour, and not out of any love toward him. The less you make him, the less he shall be able to harm you and yours; and if her majesty's favour fail him, he will again decline to a common person. For after-revenges, fear them not; for your own father was esteemed to be the contriver of Norfolk's ruin, yet his son followeth your father's son, and loveth him. Humours of men succeed not, but grow by occasions and accidents of time and power. Somerset made no revenge on the Duke of Northumberland's heirs; Northumberland that now is, thinks not of Hatton's issue; Kelloway lives that murdered the brother of Horsey; and Horsey let him go-by all his lifetime. I could name you a thousand of those; and therefore after-fears are but prophecies or rather conjectures from causes remote: look to the present, and you do wisely. His son shall be the youngest Earl of England but one; and if his father be now kept down, Will Cecil shall be able to keep as many men at his heels as he, and more too. He may also match in a better house than his; and so that fear is not worth the fearing. But if the father continue, he will be able to break the branches, and pull up the tree root and all. Lose not your advantage; if you do, I read your destiny. Let the queen hold Bothwell; while she hath him he will ever be the canker of her estate and safety. Princes are lost by security, and preserved by prevention. I have seen the last of her good days, and all ours, after his liberty.[13]

The queen was urged into action when generals and disaffected soldiers from Essex's army began causing trouble in the city. She ordered them back to their regiments and then on 29 November a pronouncement was made in the Star Chamber of the queen's displeasure over the Irish expedition. Four days later 160 servants of his household in Essex House were told to find new jobs.

The public were appeased by the pronouncement but not so Essex's friends and family. His wife Frances had tried to see the queen but had been refused. She had given birth to his daughter also called Frances in September. Behind the scenes men like Southampton were trying to work in his favour, keeping up his correspondence with the king of Scotland and considering how he could escape to France. Francis Bacon had deserted his patron but Anthony still worked diligently in the background. But for once Essex was truly ill and on 10 December he received communion and was allowed a visit from his wife. Untrue reports of his death were already flooding the city and Elizabeth sent eight of her physicians to him appalled at their reports that 'they found his liver stopped and perished ... his Intrailes and Guttes were exulcerated'.[14] The queen sent him a message that she 'meant to correct and not to ruyne'[15] him but the Privy Council were still putting together a case against him with her blessing.

Elizabeth I

Chapter Nine

The Essex Rebellion

1600–1601

Essex's family had rallied around him. His mother joined his sister Penelope and wife Frances at Essex House in January but his sister Dorothy after leaving her second husband, Henry Percy, 9th Earl of Northumberland, was residing in Putney. She corresponded with her brother telling him 'It was his Lordship's pleasure upon no cause given by me to have me keep house by myself'.[1]

Penelope had also been writing letters but angered the queen by writing to her in support of her brother.

> *... whom all men have liberty to defame as if his offence was capital and he so base dejected a creature that his love his life his service to your beauties and the state had deserved no absolution after so hard punishment, or so much as to answer in your fair presence, who would vouchsafe more justice and favour than he can expect of partial judges or those combined enemies that labour on false grounds to build his ruin, urging his faults as criminal to your divine honour, thinking it a heaven to blaspheme heaven; whereas by their own particular malice and counsel they have practised to glut themselves in their own private revenge, not regarding your service and loss so much as their ambition and to rise by his overthrow; and I have reason to apprehend that if your fair hands do not check the courses of their unbridled hate, their last courses will be his last breath...*[2]

Penelope was kept under house arrest and then brought before the Privy Council to answer for her boldness but she stood her ground and swore her fealty to the queen out of concern for her brother. A postscript she added to her letter at the time of her interview read 'I meant what I wrote and I wrote what I meant'.[3]

Penelope did not mention who exactly Essex's enemies were but would later send another letter to the queen listing them which Elizabeth burnt before Cecil could see it. He might well have been named as one who sought the earl's fall. Their mother Lettice too tried to sweeten the queen and sent her a gift of a gown worth £100 which we can be sure she never wore.

It may be now that his mother wrote to him concerned about his well-being and promising to send his stepfather Sir Christopher Blount to help him.

Swet Ro(bert) your self hath geuen me such a tast(e) of sume strang(e) matter to be loked for as I cannot be quiet tyll I know the trew caus(e) of your abcence and discontentment for it be but for Ierland I dought not but you ar(e) wyse and polytyke enufe to counter myne with your enemys whos deuelysh practyces can noe way hurt you but on wherefore my dere sonne geue me leue to be a lytle ielious ouer you for your good and intret you to have euer god and your oune honore before your ey(e)s so shall you be sure that he will dyspos inded all as you say for the best in dyspyght of all enemyse my frend (Blount) and I cannot but be trobled with thys news and doe wish out selues with you as he would sone be if we thought his sarues nedfull of that you would haue it so w(h)ich let us know and he will leue all other ocasyons what so euer and will presentlye be with you well if it be but mens matters I know you have corage enufe if womens you haue metlye well passed the pyks (pikes) allredy and therein you shuld be skyllfull so praynge you do not to be to secret from your best frends. I end beseeching the allmyghtye to bles you euer in hys highest fauoure whill I am your mother derlyest.[4]

The queen however was softening a little towards her errant

favourite. Lord Egerton's wife had died and he was unable to keep up his duties as Essex's keeper so the queen allowed the earl to return to Essex House in March after his family were removed and placed him under the care of Sir Richard Berkeley, previously Lieutenant of the Tower. Essex's trial was set for 7 February but the queen postponed it. It was a small reprieve.

Essex had, however, been communicating through his secretary, Henry Cuffe, with Charles Blount, Lord Mountjoy, by whom Penelope had now had four children. He was sent over to Ireland in February to continue the work Essex had abandoned. Essex was so frustrated at not being able to gain an audience with the queen he planned to do it by force. If Mountjoy could raise the men and perhaps be boosted by support from the King of Scotland, they could ride on London and force the queen to see him. Mountjoy had agreed to the plan as long as there was an assurance the queen would not be hurt but once he was in Ireland he changed his mind. Southampton was sent to him with a letter from Essex but to no avail. Mountjoy had other things to concern him and helping the rebellious earl was not one of them.

Essex was urged to leave any plans of using force aside and to write a flattering letter to the queen instead. In May he wrote:

Before all letters written in this hand be banished, or he that sends this enjoins himself eternal silence, be pleased, I humbly beseech your Majesty, to read over these humble lines. At sundry times I received these words as your own, 'that you meant to correct and not to ruin,' since which time, when I languished in four months' sickness, forfeited almost all that I was able to engage, felt the very pangs of death upon me, but buried and I alive, I yet kissed your fair correcting hand, and was confident in your royal word; for I said to myself, 'Between my ruin and my Sovereign's favour there is no mean, and if she bestow favour again, she gives it with all things that in this world I either need or desire.' But now that the

length of my troubles and the increase of your indignation have
made all men so afraid of me as my own poor state is ruined, and
my friends and servants like to die in prison, because I cannot help
myself with my own, I not only feel the weight of your indignation,
and am subject to their malicious informations that first envied
me your favour, and now hate me out of custom; but, as if I were
thrown into a corner like a dead carcase, I am gnawed on and torn
by the basest creatures upon earth. The prating tavern haunter
speaks of me what he lists; they print me and make me speak to the
world, and shortly they will play me upon the stage.

The least of these is worse than death, but this is not the worst
of my destiny; for you, who have protected from scorn and infamy
all to whom you once avowed favour but Essex, and never repented
of any gracious assurance you had given till now, have now, in
this eighth month of my close imprisonment, rejected my letters,
and refused to hear of me, which to traitors you never did. What
remains is only to beseech you to conclude my punishment, my
misery and my life, altogether, that I may go to my Saviour, who
has paid Himself a ransom for me, and whom (me thinks) I still
hear calling me out of this unkind world, in which I have lived too
long, and once thought myself happy.[5]

The queen was touched by his letter but it was followed by the
reissue of Essex's 'Apologie' which was now in print and widely
circulated with the addition of his sister's letter. It may have
boosted his popularity with the public but not with Elizabeth
and she allowed his trial to be held now on 5 June. Essex knelt
before 18 commissioners at York House whilst the Sergeant
reminded Essex that the queen was given to this private
tribunal in her mercy and that she had also cleared £10,000 of
his debt before he went to Ireland and had provided more for
the expedition.

Then Sir Edward Coke took over. Essex was allowed to sit
whilst he listed Essex's crimes all pertaining to his misconduct

in Ireland. The solicitor-general added that Ireland was still in a dire situation that the earl had done nothing to relieve. And then Francis Bacon, once Essex's loyal servant, closed the case with a detailed account of Essex's actions in Ireland but also quoted from a letter the earl had written two years previously and raised the issue of Hayward's book and the earl's patronage of it.

Essex was then allowed to speak. He was repentant and sorrowful, a picture of misery, but he then ruined the sympathy he was gaining by stubbornly answering each charge made against him.

The trial had lasted all day and now each commissioner rose to give his verdict. By nine in the evening, the earl was told he was now stripped of his offices and could return to Essex House but still as a prisoner until the queen decided otherwise.

Nevertheless it seemed that the queen was warming to Essex again. She read all his letters although she replied to none but Lady Scrope told him

she seemed exceedingly pleased with it yet her answer was only to will me to give you thanks for your great care to know of her health. I told her that now the time drew near of your whole year's punishment and therefore I hoped her Majesty would restore her favour to one that with so much true sorrow did desire it but she would answer me never a word bit sighed and said indeed it was so. I do not doubt but shortly to see your Lordship at court.[6]

But that perhaps was wishful thinking. Elizabeth's humour and mood concerning Essex swung one way and then another. She hated that he had made knights without her permission going as far as to wanting to denounce their knighthoods until she was persuaded otherwise. He had also mentioned during his tribunal that Leicester had once returned home without her permission but she knew he had not and anyway Leicester was in a different league to Essex. As much as he had tried, he never truly matched up to his stepfather and although Elizabeth had showered them both with affection, Leicester remained her lost love. Essex tried to twist her in ways that made her question herself and she saw that all too clearly now.

Francis Bacon too was trying to negotiate his way between his sovereign and his late patron. He wrote to Essex:

I humbly pray you to believe that I aspire to the conscience and commendation first of bonus civis, which with us is a good and true servant to the Queen, and next of bonus vir, that is an honest man. I desire your Lordship also to think that though I confess I love some things much better than I love your Lordship, as the Queen's service, her quiet and contentment, her honour, her favour, the good of my country, and the like, yet i love few persons better than yourself, both for gratitude's sa'e, and for your own virtues, which cannot hurt but by accident or abuse. Of which my good affection I was ever and am ready to yield testimony by any good offices but with such reservations as yourself cannot but allow; for as I was ever sorry that your Lordship should fly with waxen wings, doubting Icarus' fortune, so far the growing up of your own feathers, specially ostrich's, or any other save a bird of prey, no man shall be more glad... [7]

Essex did not blame him. He could do with all the supporters he could get and he wrote back 'your profession of affection, and offer of good offices, are welcome to me'.[8] There had also been more affection between the earl and his wife who was expecting another child, Dorothy, who would be born later in the year.

He was happier still when Elizabeth lifted his house arrest in August even though he was still banished from court. He had back his freedom at least but his situation was not pleasant. Debt had always been an issue for Essex and he currently owed £16,000. He planned for campaigns with gusto and great expense. He lived way beyond his means but always hoped that Elizabeth would aid him. He kept up his letters to Elizabeth hoping she would now welcome him back to court. She had done so on many occasions but not now. The renewal of his sweet wines licence came up in October and the queen did not renew it. Essex was devastated and saw that there was not much hope of ever truly returning to her favour. Still he would not give up. If only he could see her, speak to her and explain everything would be all right.

The earl may have been delusional but once he was free his supporters rallied to him at Essex House. He looked further for support from the king of Scotland, sending letters to him that denounced Cecil and Raleigh as men who would not welcome his succession to the English crown if it came to pass. As well as that Raleigh had been given the position of governor of Jersey and the earl swore he would use it as a base to allow the Spanish to invade. Essex kept James I's correspondence in a black bag tied around his neck and showed it to no one. His behaviour was becoming more erratic and more desperate. It is possible he was in the tertiary stage of syphilis, which can affect the brain in its last phase. Dr Lopez had told others he had treated him for the disease but Essex's situation was dire whether it was exacerbated by this illness or not.

In November he wrote one of his last letters to the queen about her Accession Day:

Vouchsafe, dread Sovereign, to know their lives a man though dead to the world, and in himself exercised with continued torments of mind and body, that doth more true honor to your thrice blessed day, than all those that appear in your sight. For no soul had ever such an impression of your perfections, no alteration shewed such an effect of your power, nor no heart ever felt such joy of your triumph. For they that feel the comfortable influence of your Majesty's favour, or stand in the bright beams of your presence, rejoice partly for your Majesty's, but chiefly for their own, happiness.

Only miserable Essex, full of pain, full of sickness, full of sorrow, languishing in repentance for his offences past, hateful to himself that he is yet alive, and importunate on death, if your sentence be irrevocable, he joys only for your Majesty's great happiness and happy greatness; and were the rest of his days never so many, and sure to be as happy as they are like to be miserable, he would lose them all to have this happy seventeenth day many and many times renewed with glory to your Majesty, and comfort of all your faithful subjects, of whom none is accursed but your Majesty's humble vassal.[9]

Steven W. May, in his article on 'The poems of Edward de Vere, seventeenth Earl of Oxford and Robert Devereux, second Earl of Essex' suggests this poem, possibly sent to the queen when Essex was in Ireland, may have actually been written by the earl at this time.

Happy were he could finish forth his fate
In some unhaunted desert, where, obscure
From all society, from love and hate
Of worldly folk; then might he sleep secure;
Then wake again, and ever give God praise,
Content with hip, with haws, and bramble-berry;
In contemplation passing all his days,
And change of holy thoughts to make him merry;
Who, when he dies, his tomb might be a bush,
Where harmless Robin dwells with gentle thrush.[10]

Essex House became a hotbed of malcontents, men loyal to the earl who sought change even if that meant taking radical action. The nobles who supported him were young and restless, many of them in debt and they saw a chance through Essex to rise higher in a reformed court. Men like the earls of Rutland, Southampton, Bedford and Sussex and Lord Sandys, Cromwell and Mounteagle joined forces with other discontented men including Robert Catesby and Francis Tresham who would later be involved in the Gunpowder Plot as well as men who had fought with Essex on his military campaigns.

It did not go unnoticed that Essex House was swarming with bravado and that the earl was keeping his own court. Essex received a note from Lord Treasurer Buckhurst that his behaviour was causing consternation but the earl was too far gone with his own plans to ever give up. Robert Cecil who had the queen's ear and Sir Walter Raleigh who guarded her were to blame for his inability to see the queen or so he thought. If he and his men could march on Whitehall and take custody of the queen Essex would finally be able to talk to her and Cecil and Raleigh could be dealt with.

Essex's behaviour was becoming even more unpredictable. Sir John Harington felt 'he shifted from sorrow and repentance to rage and rebellion so suddenly, as well proveth him devoid of good reason as of a right mind. His speeches of the Queen became no man who hath *mens sana in corpore sano*. He hath ill advisors, and much evil has sprung from the source ... The man's soul seems tossed to and fro, like the waves of a troubled sea'.[11]

To boost morale a special showing of Shakespeare's *Richard II* was performed reluctantly by the Lord Chamberlain's company. The play depicted the deposition of a king and it sent alarm bells ringing around the Privy Council. They could see a rebellion brewing and on Saturday 7 February Essex received a summons to meet with them. He refused on the grounds he was ill and his supporters knowing their plans were nearly exposed geared up to march through the city – apparently to be joined with 1000 London militia – before taking Whitehall.

On Sunday 8 February their plans were well underway

when four councillors, Lord Keeper Egerton, Lord Chief Justice Popham, the Earl of Worcester and Sir William Knollys, Essex's uncle, were sent to Essex House. To get to the earl they had to pass uncomfortably through 300 men arming themselves for the day ahead. Lord Keeper Egerton tried to dissuade them 'I command you all upon your allegiance to lay down your weapons and to depart, which you all ought to do being thus commanded, if you be good subjects and owe that duty to the Queen which you profess'.[12] He was lucky not to be lynched and was chased into the house by rebels intent on murder. Essex had the councillors locked inside his study – for their own protection he said – but just as much to get them out of the way.

Essex then strode out into the courtyard and rallied his men. They erupted through the gates but instead of heading straight for Whitehall where the queen was poorly defended they headed into the city to raise more support. The 1000 militia men that London sheriff, Thomas Smythe, had promised failed to materialise and the delay in trying to encourage people to join their mob gave the queen's men time to enter the city and draw a chain across the Lud Gate cutting the rebels off. The men gathered in Fenchurch Street waiting for direction but Essex had lost control and strangely called for food before sitting down to dine in the Sheriff's house. His supporters began to leave him as a proclamation was read out denouncing the earl as a traitor.

Essex wildly shouted out into the streets for his men and those left marched with him to Gracechurch Street where the sheriff asked him to give himself up to the city authorities. It was as if he had not spoken. Essex continued to call to his men and ordered the sheriff to follow him with his militia – the militia that did not exist.

They had nowhere to go but to turn back for Essex House however the Lud Gate was now defended by pikemen and they were not letting anyone through. The earl asked for passage back to his house but Captain John Leveson refused. As a stand-off ensued an eager member of Essex's band of men fired his pistol. Chaos descended. Sir Christopher Blount, Essex's stepfather, charged the chain and received a face wound before being knocked unconscious. Leveson ordered his men forward and Essex could do nothing but flee. A chain had been strung up across Friday Street barring their access to the river but local people raised the chain and the earl fell stumbling into the Thames to be aided into a boat. His only thought now was to return to Essex House and use the Privy Councillors locked in his study as hostages. If he had been thinking clearly he could have just headed for the coast and escaped.

Instead he returned home, creeping up through the garden from Essex Stairs, to find it surrounded by the Lord Admiral's men and his hostages – the councillors – had been released. Not only that but the whole area was surrounded by troops loyal to the queen and cannon were being transported from the Tower. Essex slipped through them and knowing the game was nearly up burnt any incriminating documents including the letter from the king of Scotland he wore around his neck as the Lord Admiral ordered shots to be fired at the house. Sir Robert Sidney was sent to ask Essex and his remaining men to surrender. Southampton strode out onto the roof to dictate terms but there would be no bargaining with those seen as rebels. The lord admiral did agree however for all the women to have safe passage out of the house and then if the others did not surrender they would be blown apart. Essex agreed to surrender on three conditions; that he would have a fair trial, that he would be treated civilly after his arrest and that a priest, Mister Ashton, be made available to him. Terms agreed Essex, Southampton and the others were taken into custody, first to Lambeth Palace and then to the Tower.

On Thursday 12 February Captain Thomas Lee, one of Essex's followers, was found loitering near the queen's apartments. He had planned to force the queen to release his mentor but he was arrested, tried at Newgate and executed the next day.

Essex and Southampton did not have to wait too long for their own trial and on 19 February they were escorted to Westminster Hall. Both pleaded not guilty and Essex added:

> I call God to witness, before Whom I hope shortly to appear, that I bear a true heart to her Majesty and my country, and have done nothing but that which the law of nature commanded me to do in my own defence, and which any reasonable man would have done in the like case.[13]

Sir Edward Coke led the trial and witness statements were read out. Essex was allowed to answer his charges and respond to the statements. Southampton too was allowed to speak claiming he had known nothing about a rebellion and had not drawn his sword once that day. And then Francis Bacon spoke coolly and coldly and his sharp mind pointed to the inconsistencies in Essex's replies.

> Even so your Lordship gave out in the streets that your life was sought by Lord Cobham and Sir Walter Raleigh, by this means persuading yourself, if the City had undertaken your cause, all would have gone well on your side. But the imprisoning of the Queen's Councillors, what reference had that to my Lord Cobham, Sir Walter Raleigh and the rest?[14]

Essex grew flustered and lashed out with counteraccusations. He accused Robert Cecil of dealing with Spain, railed against him but had no proof. If he had it would have put a different spin on the proceedings. Perhaps then there would be a reason for his extreme behaviour. Cecil who had been listening to the trial in secret behind a curtain now came forward and he was not pleased.

For wit I give you the pre-eminence – you have it abundantly. For nobility also I give you place – I am not noble, yet a gentleman; I am no swordsman – there also you have the odds; but I have innocence, conscience, truth and honesty to defend me against the scandal and sting of slanderous tongues, and in this Court I stand as an upright man, and your lordship as a delinquent. I protest, before God, I have loved your person and justified your virtues; and I appeal to God and the Queen, that I told her majesty your afflictions would make you a fit servant for her, attending but a fit time to move her Majesty to call you to the Court again. And had I not seen your ambitious affections inclined to usurpation, I would have gone on my knees to her Majesty to have done you good; but you have a wolf's head in a sheep's garment ... ah, my Lord, were it but your own case, the loss had been less; but you have drawn a number of noble persons and gentlemen of birth and quality into your net of rebellion, and their bloods will cry vengeance against you. For my part, I vow to God, I wish my soul had been in heaven and my body at rest that this had not been.[15]

Cecil also answered Essex's claim he had been in league with Spain. The earl had said he was told by a councillor of Cecil's plan to support the Infanta's claim to the succession. 'Name him if you dare. If you do not name him, it must be believed to be a fiction,' Cecil said.[16]

Essex immediately retorted that here was the Earl of Southampton who had also heard the rumour. He named Sir William Knollys, his uncle, who was now brought forward to answer and he agreed something was said but it was in reference to a discussion about Doleman's *Conference on the Next Succession* and Cecil had commented 'Is it not a strange impudence in that Doleman to give as equal right in the succession of the Crown to the Infanta of Spain as to any other?' Essex had been proved wrong and Cecil added 'Your malice whereby you seek to work me into hatred amongst all men, hath flowed from no other cause than from my affection to peace for the good of the country, and your own inflamed heart for war.' Then said 'I forgive you from the bottom of my heart.'[17]

Essex also said he forgave Cecil 'because I mean to die in charity with all men'. The councillors left to consider their verdict but there really was no come back for Essex this time. His peers condemned him each saying 'Guilty, my lord, of high treason, upon mine honour.'[18] The same verdict was given to Southampton who begged for mercy as Essex never would.

They were condemned to be hanged, drawn and quartered but this would be commuted to execution by axe. Elizabeth signed Essex's death warrant on the same day of the trial. Where once she had hesitated to sign a warrant, Mary Queen of Scots or Dr Lopez's, this time there was no hesitation.

Essex did not want to see any of his family – the only solace he wanted was from his priest. He did however receive a visit from Doctor Thomas Dove who tried to get him to name more conspirators but the earl would have none of it. Yet he told all to Ashton who informed the Privy Council and Cecil asked him to write down his confession. Amongst those he pointed the finger at was his sister Penelope whom once he had been so close to. 'I must accuse one who is most nearest to me, my sister, who did continually urge me on with telling how all my friends and followers thought me a coward, and that I had lost all my valour. She must be looked to, for she hath a proud spirit'.[19]

Why would he accuse Penelope now? To do so was to sign her death warrant. She may well have goaded him into action but she was not responsible for the mistakes Essex had made. They were all his own. Penelope would be placed under house arrest and questioned where she 'used herself with that modesty and wisdom as the report being made unto Her Majesty she was presently set at liberty and sent unto my lord her husband'.[20] Penelope wrote to Lord Nottingham:

It is known that I have been more like a slave than a sister, which proceeded out of my exceeding love rather than his authority... so strangely have I been wronged, as may well be an argument to make one despise the world, finding the smoke of envy where affection should be clearest.[21]

The queen at least believed she was not responsible for the rebellion.

Essex sent no apology to Elizabeth nor spoke of her. A later story told of how Elizabeth had given him a ring which if he were in dire need he should send to her and he would be forgiven. He is supposed to have passed this out of his window to a passing page boy who gave it to Lady Nottingham who kept it to herself only telling the queen he had tried to ask for her forgiveness on her death bed. But this appears to be just a romantic story to end the tale of their relationship. In reality Essex prepared himself for death and wrote his last poem (see Appendix One).

On 25 February Essex, dressed in black, was led from his chamber to the scaffold on Tower Green, praying along the way. Climbing the scaffold he addressed the gathered nobles:

I confess to the glory of God that I am a most wretched sinner and that my sins are more in number than the hairs on my head. I have bestowed my youth in wantonness, lust and uncleanness; I have been puffed up with pride, vanity and love of this wicked world's pleasures. For all which, I humbly beseech my Saviour Christ to be a mediator to the eternal Majesty for my pardon, especially for this my last sin, this great, this bloody, this crying, this infectious sin, whereby so many for love of me have been drawn to offend God, to offend their sovereign, to offend the world. I beseech God to forgive it us, and to forgive it me – most wretched of all; and I beseech her Majesty, the State, and Ministers thereof, to forgive it us. The Lord grant her Majesty a prosperous reign, and a long one, if it be His will. O Lord, bless her and the nobles and ministers of the Church and State. I beseech you and the world to have a charitable opinion of me for my intention towards her Majesty, whose death, upon my salvation and before God, I protest I never meant, nor violence to her person; yet I confess I have received an honourable trial, and am justly condemned. And I desire all the world to forgive me, even as I do freely and from my heart forgive all the world... [22]

Essex took off his gown and his ruff and told the executioner he forgave him. Kneeling at the block he prayed with the chaplain before taking off his doublet to reveal a scarlet waistcoat and said:

O God give me true humility and patience to endure to the end, and I pray you all to pray with me and for me, that when you shall see me stretch out my arms and my neck on the block, and the stroke ready to be given, it would please the Everlasting God to send down his angels to carry my soul before His Mercy Seat...O God I prostrate myself to my deserved punishment. [23]

Essex laid his head on the block, said part of Psalm 51 and then cried out 'Executioner, strike home! Come, Lord Jesus, come, Lord Jesus, and receive my soul: O Lord, into Thy hands I commend my spirit.' [24] Three blows ended this young man's life – he who sought to rise so high and fell so far.

Raleigh watched from a window as his long-time rival was put to death. But Raleigh was seen to be smoking and joking as the earl drew his final breath and the people would hate him for what they saw as a slight on their war hero, for they had loved the earl, as once the queen had done.

When Elizabeth heard the news of his death she was silent for a time then resumed playing her virginals. If she mourned the loss of her last favourite, she did not show it. Although Cecil knew she was broken.

Southampton lived out his time in the Tower and other nobles bought their way out of confinement but Sir Christopher Blount, Sir Gelly Meyrick and Henry Cuffe, Essex's secretary, were executed. Lettice, his mother, who had lost both her son and her husband, gave up any hope of ever returning to court and lived her time in the countryside at Chartley and Drayton Bassett until the age of 91.

Elizabeth survived Essex by only two years and with her death, the reign, glory and splendour of the Tudors passed into history.

Robert Devereux, 3rd Earl of Essex

Chapter Ten

The Earl's Descendants

Essex's wife was left with the care of her daughter by Philip Sidney and three of the Earl's children; Robert, Frances and Dorothy. They were now the children of a traitor and it must have been hard for Frances as well as the children to weather the stigma. Frances however remarried in 1603 and went on to have two more children with her new husband, Richard Burke, 4th Earl of Clanricarde and moved to the west of Ireland.

Robert was raised by his grandmother Lettice and educated at Eton and Merton College, Oxford. He had lost everything with his father's fall but the new King James VI and I would remember the loyalty his father had shown him. When James entered London Robert would carry the king's sword and by the following year he became the 3rd Earl of Essex after King James restored his title and removed the attainder on his father. He was also a companion to the Prince of Wales though their relationship would suffer when the prince called him the son of a traitor and Robert hit him with a tennis racket!

He married Frances Howard at the young age of 13 but during time abroad on a European tour she fell in love with Sir Robert Carr (later Earl of Somerset). Frances sought an annulment on the grounds of his physical incapacity. The case was made public and Robert defended himself by saying he was able to sleep with other women, just not she who 'reviled him, and miscalled him, terming him a cow and coward, and beast'.[1] He was made a laughing stock and was so infuriated he challenged his brother-in-law Charles Howard to a duel which the king forbade.

The annulment was granted in September 1613 but Essex and his brother were called before the Privy Council in October and spent several weeks in prison. The Howards demanded Frances' dowry back and the earl had to sell off land and borrow from his grandmother to cover the debt.

Frances married her lover in December. However Essex would sit at her trial three years later. Her husband and his family were accused of murdering one Sir Thomas Overbury and Robert as juror agreed to their death sentence. Frances confessed her guilt admitting she had poisoned Overbury with the help of one of her ladies. Her husband pleaded innocent and both were sent to the tower until 1622 when they were pardoned. Robert had had a lucky escape.

Aside from his marital woes Essex had a significant military career. He served in the wars of the Palatinate from 1620 to 1624 and in 1625 like his father he attempted to capture Cadiz. Where the 2nd earl had been successful, his son was not. The Spanish defended the harbour and the English lost both ships and men in an unmitigated disaster. He was at the surrender of Breda in June 1525 and returned to England after the death of James VI and I to meet his new king, Charles I. Essex was popular with his men as his father had been but again, like his father, would not remain high in his sovereign's esteem.

After the deaths of his mother and grandmother Essex's financial prospects improved and he leased Essex House to William Seymour, Earl of Hertford, further increasing his income, retaining just one wing for his own use.

In March 1630 Essex married Elizabeth Paulet, daughter of Sir William Paulet, of Edington, Wiltshire, a previous High Sheriff of Wiltshire. They had met through his sister Frances. She also had a lover and it seems there were also issues within this marriage. Finding his wife was pregnant, Essex said if she gave birth before 5 November, he would own the child, if born after he would disown them both. She gave birth exactly on the 5th and Essex had to claim the child was his but their son would die a month later. The earl swore he would shun women 'and put aside all hopes of a successful marriage and an heir'.[2]

They separated in 1631 with his wife staying at Essex House and the earl removing to the countryside. There were no surviving children from either of his marriages.

He served Charles I in 1639 as lieutenant-general against the Scottish – a battle that never happened but was becoming increasingly discontent. When Charles travelled to Scotland he was one of the 16 commissioners who were left in charge of the state. Charles wanted peace but others were gearing up for war. Oliver Cromwell sent an order that Essex should mobilise and command forces in the south. On Charles' return his commission was revoked but civil war was looming and on 12 July1642 Parliament resolved 'that an army shall be forthwith raised for the safety of the king's person, the defence of both the houses of parliament, and of those who have obeyed their orders and commands; and for the preservation of the true religion, the laws, liberties and peace of the kingdom. (And) resolved, that the Earl of Essex be named general thereof'.[3]

He became the first Captain-General and Chief Commander of the Parliamentarian army during the English Civil War from 1642 to 1644. In 1643 the king had moved to Oxford and Essex moved to capture him but was unsuccessful. He served at the battle of Edgehill and captured Reading in 1643 but in 1644 was sent to relieve Lyme and got caught between the queen and her army in Cornwall and Charles I and his army who were approaching behind him. By the time he reached Lostwithiel he was surrounded by royalist troops. He was expecting back-up from the Earl of Warwick who was sailing with men from Portsmouth but poor weather meant they had been able to join him.

On 21 August, Essex was attacked by Royalist troops. Charles' men outnumbered his by two to one. With no hope of fresh troops, Essex fled in a fishing boat to Plymouth leaving Sir Philip Skippon, his Sergeant Major General of Foot, in command to dictate their terms of surrender. Essex wrote 'it is the greatest blow that ever befell our party'.[4]

He resigned his commission on 2 April 1645 but was allowed a yearly payment of £10,000 for his services. On 10th September 1646 Robert fell ill whilst hunting in Windsor Park. He died on the 14th at Essex House. He was buried at Westminster Abbey and Parliament paid £5000 towards his funeral which over 3000 people attended. His effigy would later be destroyed by the order of Charles II.

As Robert died with no heirs, he was the last Earl of Essex from the Devereux line. His property and estate were left mainly to his sisters.

During his lifetime, Robert had kept close family ties with his sisters Frances and Dorothy and arranged the marriages.

Frances married Sir William Seymour, 2nd Duke of Somerset, son of Edward Seymour, Lord Beauchamp and Honora Rogers, on 3 March 1616 at Drayton Bassett – her grandmother's home. Frances was Seymour's second wife. He had previously married Arbella Stuart without permission from King James and subsequently both had been imprisoned in the Tower. They both escaped but Arbella was quickly recaptured and spent the rest of her days in captivity until her death in September 1615. Seymour however fled to Bruges and Paris until he was pardoned and allowed to return to England. Not long after he married Frances.

Little is known of Frances' life. Seymour was an avid book collector and it seems that Frances shared his passion. When Lichfield Cathedral came under siege in 1646 a volume of the eighth century Lichfield Gospels found its way to Frances, now Duchess of Somerset. After Seymour's death Frances gave 1000 books to the Cathedral Library.

Frances had seven surviving children, four sons and three daughters. She died on 24 April 1674 after living through the reigns of James I, Charles I and into the times of Charles II. She is buried in St Mary Churchyard, Great Bedwyn, Wiltshire.

Her numerous descendants include The Queen Mother and Queen Elizabeth II.

Dorothy married Sir Henry Shirley, 2nd Baronet of Staunton Harold, Co. Leicester, son of Sir George Shirley, and Frances Berkeley, on 18 May 1615 at St. Lawrence Pountney, London. Her husband was imprisoned in 1627 for an argument with the Earl of Huntingdon but he apologised and received a pardon.

Dorothy was a poet and patron of the arts. After her husband supposedly had an affair, she wrote a poem 'Of Uncon(s)tancy' which appeared in a miscellany collected by her friend Constance Aston Fowler, where she accuses him of feigning his love for her. She also 'both for safeguard of her honour, blemished by him scandalously, and for her alimony or maintenance (being glad to get from him) ... was forced to endure a suit in the High Commission Court'.[5] She took him back to court for non-payment for the maintenance she was granted.

In 1632, Thomas Fitzherbert dedicated his translation of a life of St Francis Xavier to her and praised her for her commitment to the Catholic faith to which she had remained devoted even through 'Reasons, Tryalls, & Provocations to the contrary'.[6]

James Shirley, a favourite of Queen Henrietta Maria, also dedicated *The Changes or Love in a Maze* to her with a poem:

Madam, who make the glory of your blood,
No privilege at all to be less good,
Pardon the rudeness of a comedy,
That (taught too great ambition) would fly
To kiss your white hand, and receive from thence
Both an authority, and innocence.
'Tis not this great man, nor that prince, whose fame
Can more advance a poem, than your name,
To whose clear virtue truth is bound, and we,
That there is so much left for history.
I do acknowledge custom, that to men

Such poems are presented; but my pen
Is not engag'd, nor can allow too far
A Salic law in poetry, to bar
Ladies th' inheritance of wit, whose soul
Is active, and as able to control,
As some t'usurp the chair, which write a style
To breathe the reader better than a mile.
But no such empty titles buy my flame;
Nor will I sin so much, to shew their name
In print; some servile nutses be their drudge,
That sweat to find a patron, not a judge.[7]

After her husband's death in 1633 Lucius Carey, Viscount Falkland described her as 'one of the fairest, wittiest, and newest widdowes of our time'.[8]

They had had three children; Charles, Robert and Lettice and she went on to marry William Stafford of Blatherwyck, Northants in Somerset House in 1634. This marriage also does not appear to have been happy and George Gerrard wrote to the Earl of Stafford soon after that 'they both repent it already'.[9]

She died two years after on 30 March 1636 and is buried in the church at Blatherwyck.

And then there was **Walter Devereux**, Essex's son by his mistress, Elizabeth Southwell, who had been given to his mother Lettice to raise. He was educated at Queen's College, Oxford.

Walter was close to his half-brother Robert and stood as his second when Robert challenged Henry Howard to a duel. Walter signed the *Declaration of Essex's Seconds*.

Whereas there has been a new relation of the quarrel betwixt my
Lord of Essex and Mr. Henry Howard, after his Majesty had
reconciled them, made by the four seconds before Sir Horatio Vere
and Sir John Wentworth, and the same being drawn into the brief
by Mr. Horton, one that was secretary to the last Lord Treasurer,

and we setting our hands thereto, not reading it, but only hearing it read, not mistrusting anything, but to find just dealing, have since seen a copy thereof, which we find contrary to that which was then agreed upon, and merely false in some main points; we have a sight of the original copy for our satisfaction, not to satisfy the world, for the which we do unjustly suffer a hard censure.

Be it known, therefore, to all men, that we do utterly disclaim from any such writing. And whereas we have been hitherto tender and sparing of their reputations, now, finding that they have put this trick upon us, we do publish to the world no writing but the first to be true - to which we have only set our hands - and they have acknowledged to be true before Sir Horatio Vere and Sir Jno. Wentworth, and at divers other times to others; and so true, as they neither can nor dare deny it, in which is plain to be seen they might have fought if they would. And thus much we will be ready to justify, upon the sacrament first, and then with our swords.[11]

Walter was sent to the Fleet prison with his brother to cool off but remained loyal to the 3rd Earl. Robert helped him to obtain a position at King James I court and he was knighted in 1617. He also served as a member for Parliament between 1614 and 1641.

Walter acted as his agent when Robert served in the Palatinate and in 1624 was a captain of the foot in Essex's regiment during action in the Low Countries and the siege of Breda. He returned to England in 1625 and continued to serve Robert.

When the earl suspected his second wife of having an affair Walter found evidence she was meeting with Sir William Uvedale. Although his grandmother tried to arrange a marriage for Walter it is not certain that he ever had a wife.

He died at Essex House on 26 July 1641 and was buried in the church of St. Clement Danes.

Appendix One

His Last Poem

From silent night, true register of moans,
From saddest Soul consumed with deepest sins,
From heart quite rent with sighs and heavy groans,
My wailing Muse her woeful work begins.
And to the world brings tunes of sad despair,
Sounding nought else but sorrow, grief and care.

Sorrow to see my sorrow's cause augmented,
And yet less sorrowful were my sorrows more:
Grief that my grief with grief is not prevented,
For grief it is must ease my grieved sore.
Thus grief and sorrow cares but how to grieve,
For grief and sorrow must my cares relieve.

The wound fresh bleeding must be staunched with tears
Tears cannot come unless some grief precede;
Griefs come but slack, which doth increase my fears.
Fears, lest for want of help I still should bleed.
Do what I can to lengthen my life's breath,
If tears be wanting, I shall bleed to death.

Thou, deepest searcher of each secret thought,
Infuse in me thy all-affecting grace;
So shall my works to good effects be brought,
While I peruse my ugly sins a space,
Whose staining filth so spotted hath my soul,
As nought will wash but tears of inward dole.

Oh that the learned poets of this time

(who in a love-sick line so well indite)
Would not consume good wit in hateful rhyme,
But would with care some better subject write:
For if their music please in earthly things,
Well would it sound if strained with heavenly strings.

But woe it is to see fond worldlings use,
Who most delight in things that vainest be;
And without fear work virtue's foul abuse,
Scorning soul's rest and all true piety,
As if they made account never to part
From this frail life, the pilgrimage of smart.

Such is the nature of our foolish kind,
When practiced sin hath deeply taken root,
The way to penance due is hard to find,
Repentance held a thing of little boot;
For contrite tears, soul's health, and angels'
Most men account a mere fantastic toy.

Ill-working use, devourer of all grace,
The fretting moth that wasteth soul's chief bliss,
The sly close thief that lurks in every place,
Filching by piece-meal, till the whole be his;
How many are deceived by thy bait,
T'account their sins as trifles of no weight?

Oh cursed custom, causing mischief still,
Too long thy craft my senses hath misled;
Too long have I been slave unto thy will,
Too long my soul on bitter sweets hath fed;
Now surfeiting with thy hell poisoned cates,
In deep repent, her former folly hates.

And humbly comes with sorrow rented heart,
With blubbered eyes, and hands up-reared to heaven
To play a poor lamenting Maudlin's part,
That would weep streams of blood to be forgiven;
But oh, I fear mine eyes are drained so dry,
That though I would, yet now I cannot cry.

If any eye therefore can spare a tear
To fill the well-spring that must wet my cheeks,
O let that eye to this sad feast draw near,
Refuse me not my humble soul beseeks:
For all the tears mine eyes have ever wept
Were now too little had they all been kept.

I see my sins arraigned before my face
I see their number pass the moths in sun.
I see that my continuance in this place
Cannot be long, and all that I have done,
I see before my face the judge hath laid,
At whose stern looks all creatures are afraid.

If he be just my soul condemned is,
And just he is; what then may be expected,
But banishment from everlasting bliss?
To live like cursed Cain, base, vile, abjected;
He in his rage his brother's blood did spill;
I more unkind mine own soul's life do kill.

O could mine eyes send trickling tears amain,
Never to cease till my eternal night,
Till this eye flood his mercy might obtain,
Whom my defaults have banished from his sight;
Then could I bless my happy time of crying,
But ah, too soon my barren springs are drying.

Thrice happy sinner was that blessed saint,
Who though he fell with puff of woman's blast,
Went forth and wept with many a bitter plaint.
And by his tears obtained grace at last;
But wretched I have fallen of mine accord,
Ten thousand times against the living Lord.

Yet cannot strain one true repentant tear,
To gain the bliss from which my soul is banished;
My flinty heart such sorrowing doth forebear,
And from my sense all true remorse is vanished;
For heart and sense are cloyed with dregs of sin,
And there's no place for Grace to enter in.

No place (dear Lord) unless thy goodness please
To pity him that worst deserves of any,
And in thy tender mercy showed to many;
Yet none of those do equal me in sin,
Oh how may I hope mercy then to win?

The traitor Judas, heir born to perdition,
Who for a trifle did his Lord betray,
In equal doom deserveth more remission,
Then my defaults can challenge any way;
He sold him once, that once for gain was done;
I oftentimes, yet than nothing won.

The bloody-minded Jews, in fury mad,
Until on Christ their cruel rage was fed,
In their fell anger more compassion had
Than I, for whom his harmless blood was shed;
Their hellish spite within a day was past,
My sinful fit doth all my lifetime last.

For every stripe that he from them did take,
A thousand deadly sins have I committed;
And every sin as deep a wound did make,
As did the cords wherewith my Christ was whipped;
Oh hateful caitiff, parricide most vile,
Thus (with my sin) his pure blood to defile.

O sin, first parent of man's ever woe,
The distance large that severs hell and heaven;
Sense's confounded, soul's chief overthrow,
Grafted by men, not by the grafter given;
Consuming canker, wasting soul's chief treasure,
Only to gain a little trifling pleasure.

Happy were man if sin had never been,
Thrice happy now, if sin he would forsake,
But happier far, if for his wicked sin
He would repent, and hearty sorrow make;
Leaving this dross and fleshy delectation,
To gain in heaven a lasting habitation.

There is the place wherein all sorrows die,
Where joy exceeds all joy that ever were;
Where angels make continual harmony,
The mind set free from care, distrust, or fear;
There all receive all joyful contention,
Happied by that most heavenly contemplation.

Now see (alas) the change we make for sin,
Instead of heaven, hell is become our lot;
For blessed saints, damned fiends we ever win;
For rest and freedom, lasting bondage got;
For joy, content, eternal love and peace,
Grief, despair, hate, and jars that never cease.

The worm of conscience still attendeth on us,
Telling each hour, each instant we shall die,
And that our sins cannot be parted from us,
But where we are, thither they likewise fly;
Still urging this, that death we have deserved,
Because we fled from him we should have served.

What greater sin can touch a human heart?
What hellish fury can be worse tormented?
What sinner lives that feeleth not a part
Of this sharp plague, unless he have repented?
And yet repentance surely is but vain,
Without full purpose not to sin again.

And is it not then our plain folly's error,
To covet that that brings with it contempt,
And makes us live in fear, disgust, and terror,
Hating at last the thing we did attempt?
For never sin did yet so pleasing taste,
But lustful flesh did loathe it when t'was past.

Witness my woeful soul, which well can tell,
In highest hope of sin's most fresh delight,
Although my frailty suffered me to dwell,
Yet being past, I loathed it with despight;
But like the swine, I fed mine own desire,
That being clean, still coveteth the mire.

So greedy is man'sd beastly appetite,
To follow after dunghill pleasures still,
And feed on carrion like the ravening kite,
Not caring what his hungry maw doth fill,
But worketh evermore his will's effect,
Without restraint, controlment or respect.

O why should man, that bears the stamp of heaven,
So much abase heaven's holy will and pleasure?
O, why was sense and reason to him given,
That in his sin cannot contain a measure?
He knows he must account for every sin,
And yet committeth sins that countless been.

This to peruse (dear God) doth kill my soul,
But that thy mercy quickeneth it again;
O hear me, Lord, in bitterness of dole,
That of my sins do prostrate here complain;
And at thy feet with Mary, knock for grace,
Though wanting Marie's tears to wet my face.

She, happy sinner, saw her life misled,
At sight whereof her inward heart did bleed,
To witness which her outward tears were shed,
O blessed saint, and o most blessed deed;
But wretched I, that see more sins than she,
Nor grieve within, nor yet weep outwardly.

When she had lost thy presence but one day,
The want was such, her heart could not sustain;
But to thy tomb alone she took her way,
And there with sighs and tears she did complain;
Nor from her sense once moved or stirred was she,
Until again she got a sight of thee.

But I have lost thy presence all my days,
And still am slack to seek thee as I should;
My wretched soul in wicked sin so stays,
I am unmet to see thee, though I would;
Yet if I could with tears thy coming tend,
I know I should (as she) find thee my friend.

Tears are the key that ope the way to bliss,
The holy water quenching heaven's quick fire,
The atonement true twixt God and our amiss,
The angels' drink, the blessed saints' desire,
The joy of Christ, the balm of grieved heart,
The spring of life, the ease of every smart.

The second king of Israel by succession,
When with Uriah's wife he had offended,
In bitter tears bewailed his great transgression,
And by his tears found grace, and so repented;
He night and day in weeping did remain,
I night nor day, to shed one tear take pain.

And yet my sins in greatness and in number,
Far his exceed; how comes it then to pass,
That my repentance should so far be under,
And grace's force, dear God, is as it was?
Truth is, that I, although I have more need,
Do not, as he, so truly weep indeed.

O wherefore is my steely heart so hard?
Why am I made of metal unrelenting?
Why is all ghostly comfort from me barred?
Or, to what end do I defer repenting?
Can lustful flesh, or flattering world persuade me,
That I can 'scape the power of him that made me?

No, no, the secret searcher of all hearts,
Both sees and knows each deed that I have done,
And for each deed will pay me home with smart,
No place can serve his will decreed to shun,
I should deceive myself to think that he
For sin would punish others, and not me.

Our first born sir, first breeder of man's thrall,
For one bare sin was of perfection reft,
And all mankind were banished by his fall
From Paradise, and unto sorrow left;
If he for one, and all for him feel pain,
Then for so many, what should I sustain?

The angels made to attend on God in glory,
Were thrust from heaven, and only for one sin;
That but in thought (for so records the story),
For which they still in lasting darkness been;
If those, once glorious, thus tormented by,
I (basest slave) what will become of me?

What will become of me, that not in thought,
In thought alone, but in each word and deed,
A thousand thousand deadly sins have wrought,
And still do work, whereat my heart doth bleed?
For even now, in this my sad complaining,
With new-made sins, my flesh my soul is staining.

O that I were removed to some close cave,
Where all alone retired from delight,
I might my sighs and tears untroubled have,
And never come in wretched worldlings' sight;
Whose ill-bewitching company still brings
Deep provocation, whence great danger springs.

Ill company, the cause of many woes,
The sugared bait, that hideth poisoned hook;
The rock unseen that ship-wracked souls o'erthrows,
The weeping crocodile that kills with look,
The readiest step to ruin and decay,
Grace's confounder, and hell's nearest way.

How many souls do perish by thy guile?
How many men without all fear frequent
Thy deadly haunts, where they in pleasure smile,
Taking no care such dangers to prevent?
But live like Beliels, unbridled or untamed,
Not looking they shall for their faults be blamed.

Alas, alas, too wretched do we live,
That carelessly doth work our own confusion,
And to our wills such liberty do give;
Ay me, it is the devil's mere illusion,
To flatter us with such sense-pleasing trains,
That he thereby may take us in his chains.

This well foresaw good men of ancient time,
Which made them shun th' occasions of foul sin,
Knowing it was the nurse of every crime,
And siren-like would train fond worldlings in;
Alluring them with show of music's sound,
Until on sin's deep shelf their souls be drowned.

But he is held no sociable man
In this corrupted age, that shall refuse
To keep accursed company now and then;
Nay but a fool, unless he seem to choose
Their fellowship, and give them highest place,
That vildest live, and furthest off from grace.

But better t'is, believe me in my trial,
To shun hell-hounds, factors of the devil,
And give them leave to grudge at your denial,
Than to partake with such in sin and evil;
For if that God (in Justice) then should slay us,
From hell and horror, who (alas) could stay us?

Good God, the just (as he himself hath spoken),
Should scarce be saved, o terror unremovable;
What then should they that never had a token,
Or sign of grace (soul's comfort most behoveable),
But graceless lived, and all good deeds did hate;
What hope of them that live in such a state?

O who will give me tears that I may wail
Both nights and days the dangers I have passed?
My soul, my soul, 'tis much for thy avail,
That thou art gotten from these straits at last;
O joy, but in thy joy mix tears withal,
That thou hast time to say, Lord hear me call.

I might as others (Lord) have perished,
Amid my sins and damnable delights;
But thou (good God) with care my soul hast cherished,
And brought me home to look on heavenly lights;
Ay me, what thanks, what service can I render
To thee that of my safety art so tender?

Now do I curse the time I ever went
In sin's black path, that leadeth to damnation;
Now do I hate the hours I have mis-spent
In idle vice, neglecting soul's salvation;
And to redeem the time I have mis-worn,
I wish this hour, I were again new-born.

But vain it is, as saith the wisest man.
To call again the day that once is past,
O let me see what best is for me then,
To gain thy favour whilst my life doth last;
That in the next I may but worthy be,
Ev'n in the meanest place to wait on thee.

I will, as did the prodigal son sometime,
Upon my knees with hearty true contrition,
And weeping eyes, confess my former crime,
And humbly beg upon my low submission,
That thou will not of former faults detect me,
But like a loving father now respect me.

Or as the wife that hath her husband wronged,
So will I come with fear and blushing cheek,
For giving others what to thee belonged,
And say, "My King, my Lord, and Spouse most meek,
I have defiled the bed that thou didst owe;
Forgive me this, it shall no more be so."

Yet, for the world can witness mine abuse,
I'll hide my face from face that witched mine eyes;
These graceless eyes, that had my body's use,
Till it be withered with my very cries,
That when my wrinkles shall my sorrows tell,
The world may say, I joy'd not, though I fell.

And thus will I in sorrowing spend my breath,
And spot my face with never-dying tears,
Till aged wrinkles, messengers of death,
Have purchased mercy and removed my fears;
And then the world within my looks shall read,
The piteous wrack, unbridled sin hath bred.

And that which was a pleasure to behold,
 Shall be to me an ever-griping pain;
All my misdeeds shall one and one be told,
That I may see what tyrants have me slain;
And when I have thus mustered them apart,
I will display on each a bleeding heart.

And lest my tears should fail me at most need,
Before my face I'll fix my saviour's passion,
And see how his most precious side did bleed,
And note his death and torments in such fashion
As never man the like did undertake,
For freely he hath done it for my sake.

If this his kindness and his mercy shown,
Cannot provoke me unto tender crying,
Then will I back again turn to mine own,
Mine own sins, cause of this his cruel dying;
And if for them no tears mine eyes can find,
Sighs shall cause tears, tears make my poor eyes blind.

No far-fetched story have I now brought home,
Nor taught to speak more language than his mother's,
No long done poem is from darkness come
To light again, it's ill to fetch from others;
The song I sing, is made from heart-bred sorrow,
Which pensive muse from pining soul doth borrow.

I sing not not I, of wanton love-sick lays,
Of trickling toys to feed fantastic ears,
My muse respects no flattering tattling praise,
A guilty conscience this sad passion bears;
My sin-sick soul, with sorrow woebegone,
Lamenting thus a wretched deed mis-done.

References

Chapter One: The Early Years

1. Margetts, 'The Birth Date of Robert Devereux, 2nd Earl of Essex'
2. Watkins, *Lady Katherine Knollys*
3. Webb, Alfred, *A Compendium of Irish Biography*
4. Ibid.
5. 'Transactions of the Leicestershire Architectural and Archaeological Society'
6. CSP Spain
7. Ibid.
8. Ibid.
9. Emerson, *Wives and Daughters: The Women of Sixteenth Century England*
10. Jenkins, *Elizabeth & Leicester*
11. *Leicester's Commonwealth*
12. Brewer and Bullen, *Calendar of the Carew Manuscripts*
13. Ibid.
14. Devereux, *Lives and Letters*
15. Ibid.
16. Ibid.
17. Ibid.
18. Aikin, *Memoirs of the Court of Elizabeth, Queen of England*
19. *Leicester's Commonwealth*
20. Devereux, *Lives and Letters*
21. Ibid.
22. Ibid.
23. Lansdowne MS 24
24. St Clare Byrne, *Elizabethan Life in Town and Country*
25. Devereux, *Lives and Letters*
26. Devereux, *An Apologie of the Earl of Essex*
27. HMSO, *Manuscripts of the Marquess of Bath*

28. Gristwood, *Elizabeth & Leicester*
29. Jenkins, *Elizabeth & Leicester*
30. Freedman, *Poor Penelope*
31. Ibid.
32. Lansdowne MS 885
33. Ellis, *Original Letters Illustrative of English History*
34. Historical Manuscripts Commission, *Manuscripts of the Marquess of Bath*
35. BL Add MS 32092 f.48
36. Devereux, *Lives and Letters*
37. Ibid.
38. Ibid.

Chapter Two: Essex's First Command

1. De Havilland, *Rome's Outworks*
2. Gristwood, *Elizabeth & Leicester*
3. Ibid.
4. Luke, *Gloriana: The Years of Elizabeth I*
5. Lacey, *Robert, Earl of Essex*
6. Devereux, *Lives and Letters*
7. Wilson, *Sweet Robin*
8. Devereux, *Lives and Letters*
9. Raleigh, *The Poems of Sir Walter Raleigh*
10. Lacey, *Robert, Earl of Essex*
11. Hammer, *The Polarisation of Elizabethan Politics*
12. St Clare Byrne, *Elizabethan Life in Town and Country*
13. Devereux, *Lives and Letters*
14. Trevelyan, *Sir Walter Raleigh*
15. Ibid.
16. Hammer, *The Polarisation of Elizabethan Politics*
17. Padel, *Sir Walter Ralegh*

Chapter Three: The Spanish Threat

1. Devereux, *Lives and Letters*

2. Aikin, *Memoirs of the Court of Elizabeth, Queen of England*
3. Wilson, *Sweet Robin*
4. Harrison, *The Life and Death of Robert Devereux Earl of Essex*
5. St Clare Byrne, *Elizabethan Life in Town and Country*
6. Freedman, *Poor Penelope*
7. Lacey, *Robert, Earl of Essex*
8. Devereux, *Lives and Letters*
9. Lacey, *Robert, Earl of Essex*
10. Ibid.
11. Strachey, *Elizabeth and Essex*
12. Hammer, *The Polarisation of Elizabethan Politics*
13. Devereux, *Lives and Letters*
14. Spenser, *The Works of Edmund Spenser*
15. Freedman, *Poor Penelope*
16. HMC Salisbury
17. Hammer, *The Polarisation of Elizabethan Politics*
18. Ibid.
19. Varlow, *The Lady Penelope*
20. Devereux, *Lives and Letters*
21. Bevington, *George Peele*
22. https://en.wikisource.org/wiki/Muses_no_more_but_mazes

Chapter Four: The French Campaign

1. Hammer, *The Polarisation of Elizabethan Politics*
2. Devereux, *Lives and Letters*
3. Guy, *Elizabeth: The Forgotten Years*
4. Varlow, *The Lady Penelope*
5. Devereux, *Lives and Letters*
6. Ibid.
7. Lacey, *Robert, Earl of Essex*
8. Guy, *Elizabeth: The Forgotten Years*
9. Doran, *Elizabeth I & Her Circle*
10. Devereux, *Lives and Letters*

11. Ibid.
12. Ibid.
13. Doran, *Elizabeth I & Her Circle*
14. Lacey, *Robert, Earl of Essex*
15. Devereux, *Lives and Letters*
16. Trevelyan, *Sir Walter Raleigh*
17. Nicholl, *The Reckoning*
18. Trevelyan, *Sir Walter Raleigh*

Chapter Five: The Lopez Plot

1. Devereux, *Lives and Letters*
2. Bacon, *The Works of Francis Bacon*
3. Du Maurier, *Golden Lads*
4. Hammer, *The Polarisation of Elizabethan Politics*
5. Green, *The Double Life of Doctor Lopez*
6. CSP Domestic – Edward VI, Mary and Elizabeth
7. Harrison, *The Life and Death of Robert Devereux Earl of Essex*
8. Hammer, *The Polarisation of Elizabethan Politics*
9. Historical Manuscripts Commission, *Manuscripts of the Marquess of Bath*
10. Guy, *Elizabeth: The Forgotten Years*
11. Bacon, *The Works of Francis Bacon*
12. Ibid.
13. Harrison, *The Life and Death of Robert Devereux Earl of Essex*
14. Du Maurier, *Golden Lads*
15. Ibid.
16. Green, *The Double Life of Doctor Lopez*
17. Ibid.
18. Whitelock, *Elizabeth's Bedfellows*
19. Green, *The Double Life of Doctor Lopez*
20. Du Maurier, *Golden Lads*
21. Green, *The Double Life of Doctor Lopez*
22. Du Maurier, *Golden Lads*
23. Strachey, *Elizabeth and Essex*

24. Bacon, *The Works of Francis Bacon*
25. Green, *The Double Life of Doctor Lopez*
26. Ibid.
27. Ibid.
28. Ibid.
29. Daybell, *Women Letter Writers in Tudor England*

Chapter Six: A Voyage to Cadiz

1. Devereux, *Lives and Letters*
2. Ibid.
3. Du Maurier, *Golden Lads*
4. Harrison, *The Life and Death of Robert Devereux Earl of Essex*
5. Parsons, *A Conference about the Next Succession to the Crown of England*
6. Ibid.
7. http://fly.hiwaay.net/~paul/bacon/devices/loveintro.html
8. ibid.
9. Lacey, *Robert, Earl of Essex*
10. Harrison, *The Life and Death of Robert Devereux Earl of Essex*
11. Strachey, *Elizabeth and Essex*
12. Doran, *Elizabeth I & Her Circle*
13. Devereux, *Lives and Letters*
14. Ibid.
15. Bacon, *The Works of Francis Bacon*
16. Ibid.
17. Devereux, *Lives and Letters*
18. Strachey, *Elizabeth and Essex*

Chapter Seven: To the Azores

1. Tytler, *Life of Sir Walter Raleigh*
2. Varlow, *The Lady Penelope*
3. Doran, *Elizabeth I & Her Circle*
4. CSP Domestic – Edward VI, Mary and Elizabeth
5. Lacey, *Robert, Earl of Essex*

6. Guy, *Elizabeth: The Forgotten Years*
7. Padel, *Sir Walter Ralegh*
8. Doran, *Elizabeth I & Her Circle*
9. Harrison, *The Life and Death of Robert Devereux Earl of Essex*
10. HMC Salisbury
11. Freedman, *Poor Penelope*
12. Graves, *Burghley: William Cecil, Lord Burghley*
13. Lindberg, 'A torch borne in the wind: the cultural persona of Robert Devereux, 2nd Earl of Essex'
14. Devereux, *An Apologie of the Earl of Essex*
15. Strachey, *Elizabeth and Essex*
16. Ibid.
17. CSP Domestic – Edward VI, Mary and Elizabeth
18. Harrison, *The Life and Death of Robert Devereux Earl of Essex*
19. Connolly and Hopkins, *Essex: The Cultural Impact of an Elizabethan Courtier*
20. Devereux, *Lives and Letters*
21. Harrison, *The Life and Death of Robert Devereux Earl of Essex*
22. Varlow, *The Lady Penelope*
23. CSP Domestic – Edward VI, Mary and Elizabeth
24. Trevelyan, *Sir Walter Raleigh*

Chapter Eight: Essex's Final Command

1. Hammer, *The Polarisation of Elizabethan Politics*
2. Harrison, *The Life and Death of Robert Devereux Earl of Essex*
3. Devereux, *Lives and Letters*
4. Ibid.
5. Ibid.
6. Bacon, *The Works of Francis Bacon*
7. Harrison, *The Life and Death of Robert Devereux Earl of Essex*
8. Lacey, *Robert, Earl of Essex*
9. HMC Salisbury
10. Devereux, *Lives and Letters*
11. Bacon, *The Works of Francis Bacon*

12. CSP Domestic – Edward VI, Mary and Elizabeth
13. Tytler, *Life of Sir Walter Raleigh*
14. Lacey, *Robert, Earl of Essex*
15. Doran, *Elizabeth I & Her Circle*

Chapter Nine: The Essex Rebellion
1. Daybell, *Women Letter Writers in Tudor England*
2. Freedman, *Poor Penelope*
3. Ibid.
4. Daybell, *Women Letter Writers in Tudor England*
5. Guy, *Elizabeth: The Forgotten Years*
6. Whitelock, *Elizabeth's Bedfellows*
7. Bacon, *The Works of Francis Bacon*
8. Ibid.
9. Devereux, *Lives and Letters*
10. Padel, *Sir Walter Ralegh*
11. Trevelyan, *Sir Walter Raleigh*
12. Lacey, *Robert, Earl of Essex*
13. Ibid.
14. Jardine, *The Lives and Criminal Trials of Celebrated Men*
15. Ibid.
16. Ibid.
17. Harrison, *A Last Elizabethan Journal*
18. Jardine, *The Lives and Criminal Trials of Celebrated Men*
19. Connolly and Hopkins, *Essex: The cultural impact of an Elizabethan courtier*
20. Freedman, *Poor Penelope*
21. Ibid.
22. Jardine, *The Lives and Criminal Trials of Celebrated Men*
23. Ibid.
24. Ibid.

Chapter Ten: The Earl's Descendants
1. Howell, *A Complete Collection of State Trials and Proceedings*

2. Snow, *Essex the rebel*
3. Ibid.
4. Ibid.
5. Howell, *A Complete Collection of State Trials and Proceedings*
6. Ibid.
7. Shirley, *The Dramatic Works and Poems of J. Shirley*
8. Wiseman, *Early Modern Women and the Poem*
9. Snow, *Essex the rebel*
10. Devereux, *Lives and Letters*

Select Bibliography

Aikin, Lucy, *Memoirs of the Court of Elizabeth, Queen of England*, New York, 1870

Bacon, Francis, *The Works of Francis Bacon*, Cambridge, 2011

Beer, Anna, *Bess: The Life of Lady Ralegh, Wife to Sir Walter*, London, 2004

Bevington, David, *George Peele*, London, 2017

BL Add MS 32092 f.48

Brewer and Bullen (eds), *Calendar of the Carew Manuscripts, 1515–1603*, 4 vols, London, 1867

Calendar of State Papers, Spain

Connolly, Annaliese & Hopkins, Lisa (eds), *Essex: The cultural impact of an Elizabethan courtier*, Manchester, 2013

Coote, Stephen, *A Play of Passion: The Life of Sir Walter Ralegh*, London, 1993

Daybell, James, *Women Letter Writers in Tudor England*, Oxford, 2006

De Havilland, Charles Richard, *Rome's Outworks; or, Our controversy with Rome*, London, 1851

Devereux, Robert, *An Apologie of the Earl of Essex Against Those which Falsely and Maliciously Tax Him to be the Only Hindrance of the Peace and Quietness of His Country*, 1598

Devereux, William Bourchier, *Lives and Letters of the Devereux, Earls of Essex*, Vol I & II, London, 1853

Doran, Susan, *Elizabeth I & Her Circle*, Oxford, 2015

Du Maurier, Daphne, *Golden Lads: Sir Francis Bacon, Anthony Bacon, and Their Friends*, London, 2013

Ellis, Henry (ed.), *Original Letters Illustrative of English History; Including Numerous Royal Letters : from Autographs in the British Museum, and One Or Two Other Collections with Notes and Illustrations*, Second Series, Volume 3, London, 1827

Emerson, Kathy Lynn, *Wives and Daughters: The Women of*

Sixteenth Century England, New York, 1984

Freedman, Sylvia, *Poor Penelope: Lady Penelope Rich, an Elizabethan woman*, Bourne End, 1983

Graves, Michael A R, *Burghley: William Cecil, Lord Burghley*, London, 1998

Green, Dominic, *The Double Life of Doctor Lopez*, London, 2003

Gristwood, Sarah, *Elizabeth & Leicester*, London, 2007

Guy, John, *Elizabeth: The Forgotten Years*, London, 2016

Hammer, Paul E J, *The Polarisation of Elizabethan Politics: The Political career of Robert Devereux, 2nd Earl of Essex, 1585–1597*, Cambridge, 1999

Harrison, G B, *A Last Elizabethan Journal*, London, 1999

Harrison, G B, *The Life and Death of Robert Devereux Earl of Essex*, Bath, 1970

Hibbert, Christopher, *The Virgin Queen: A Portrait of Elizabeth I*, London, 1990

Historical Manuscripts Commission, *Manuscripts of the Marquess of Bath, Volume V, Talbot, Dudley and Devereux Papers 1533–1659*, London, 1980

Historical Manuscripts Commission, *Manuscripts of the Most Honourable the Marquess of Salisbury*, London, 1883

Howell, Thomas Bayly, *A Complete Collection of State Trials and Proceedings for High Treason and Other Crimes and Misdemeanors: From the Earliest Period to the Year 1783, with Notes and Other Illustrations*, London, 1816

Hutchinson, Robert, *Elizabeth's Spymaster*, London, 2006

Jardine, David, *The Lives and Criminal Trials of Celebrated Men*, Philadelphia, 1835

Jenkins, Elizabeth, *Elizabeth & Leicester*, London, 1961

Kane, Brendan and McGowan-Doyle, Valerie (eds), *Elizabeth I and Ireland*, Cambridge, 2014

Lacey, Robert, *Robert, Earl of Essex: An Elizabethan Icarus*, London, 1971

Lacey, Robert, *Sir Walter Ralegh*, London, 1973

Lansdowne MS 24, MS 885

Leicester's Commonwealth, London, 1641

Lindberg, K D, 'A torch borne in the wind: the cultural persona of Robert Devereux, 2nd Earl of Essex', PhD dissertation, Ohio, 2001

Loades, David, *The Cecils*, London, 2012

Luke, Mary, *Gloriana: the years of Elizabeth I*, new York, 1973

Marcus, Leah S, Muller, Janel & Rose, Mary Beth (eds), *Elizabeth I: Collected Works*, Chicago, 2000

Margetts, Michele, 'The Birth Date of Robert Devereux, 2nd Earl of Essex', Notes & Queries; Mar1988, Vol. 35 Issue 1, p34

May, Steven W., 'The poems of Edward de Vere, seventeenth Earl of Oxford and Robert Devereux, second Earl of Essex' in Studies in Philology, 77 (Winter 1980), Chapel Hill, p.92.

Nicholl, Charles, *The Reckoning: The Murder of Christopher Marlowe*, London, 1992

Quinn, D B, *Raleigh & The British Empire*, New York, 1962

Padel, Ruth, *Sir Walter Ralegh*, London, 2010

Parsons, Robert, *A Conference about the Next Succession to the Crown of England: Divided Into Two Parts. The First Containeth the Discourse of a Civil Lawyer; How, and in what Manner Propinquity of Bloud is to be Preferred. The Second Containeth the Speech of a Temporal Lawyer, about the Particular Titles of All Such as Do, Or May Pretend ... to the Next Succession. Whereunto is Also Added, a New and Perfect Arbor and Genealogy of the Descents of All the Kings and Princes of England ...*, London, 1681

Raleigh, Sir Walter, *The Poems of Sir Walter Raleigh Collected and Authenticated with Those of Sir Henry Wotton and Other Courtly Poets from 1540 To 1650*, London, 1951

Ronald, Susan, *The Pirate Queen: Queen Elizabeth I, her Pirate Adventurers and the Dawn of Empire*, New York, 2008

Rowse, A L, *Ralegh and the Throckmortons*, London, 1962

Shirley, James, *The Dramatic Works and Poems of J. Shirley*, London,

1833

Snow, Vernon F, *Essex the rebel; the life of Robert Devereux, the third Earl of Essex, 1591-1646*, Nebraska, 1970

Spenser, *The Works of Edmund Spenser*, Vol 7, Michigan, 1943

Starkey, David, *Elizabeth*, London, 2000

Strachey, Lytton, *Elizabeth and Essex*, London, 1928

St. Clare Byrne, Muriel, *Elizabethan Life in Town and Country*, Gloucester, 1925

'Transactions of the Leicestershire Architectural and Archaeological Society', Volume 2, The Society, Leicestershire, 1870

Trevelyan, Raleigh, *Sir Walter Raleigh*, London, 2002

Tytler, Patrick Fraser, *Life of Sir Walter Raleigh: Founded on Authentic and Original Documents, Some of Them Never Before Published: Including a View of the Most Important Transations in the Reigns of Elizabeth and James I ...*, Edinburgh, 1844

Varlow, Sally, *The Lady Penelope: The Lost Tale of Love and Politics in the Court of Elizabeth I*, London, 2014

Webb, Alfred, *A Compendium of Irish Biography: Comprising Sketches of Distinguished Irishmen, and of Eminent Persons Connected With Ireland by Office or by Their Writings*, Dublin, 1878

Weir, Alison, *Elizabeth the Queen*, London, 1998

Whitelock, Anna, *Elizabeth's Bedfellows*, London, 2013

Wilson, A N, *The Elizabethans*, London, 2012

Wilson, Derek A, *Sweet Robin: A Biography of Robert Dudley, Earl of Leicester, 1533-1588*, London 1981

Wiseman, Susan, *Early Modern Women and the Poem*, Oxford, 2016

CHRONOS
BOOKS

HISTORY

Chronos Books is an historical non-fiction imprint. Chronos
publishes real history for real people; bringing to life people,
places and events in an imaginative, easy-to-digest and
accessible way - histories that pass on their stories to a
generation of new readers.
If you have enjoyed this book, why not tell other readers by
posting a review on your preferred book site.

Recent bestsellers from Chronos Books are:

Lady Katherine Knollys
The Unacknowledged Daughter of King Henry VIII
Sarah-Beth Watkins
A comprehensive account of Katherine Knollys' questionable
paternity, her previously unexplored life in the Tudor court
and her intriguing relationship with Elizabeth I.
Paperback: 978-1-78279-585-8 ebook: 978-1-78279-584-1

Cromwell was Framed
Ireland 1649
Tom Reilly
Revealed: The definitive research that proves the Irish nation
owes Oliver Cromwell a huge posthumous apology for
wrongly convicting him of civilian atrocities in 1649.
Paperback: 978-1-78279-516-2 ebook: 978-1-78279-515-5

Why The CIA Killed JFK and Malcolm X
The Secret Drug Trade in Laos
John Koerner
A new groundbreaking work presenting evidence that the CIA
silenced JFK to protect its secret drug trade in Laos.
Paperback: 978-1-78279-701-2 ebook: 978-1-78279-700-5

The Disappearing Ninth Legion
A Popular History
Mark Olly
The Disappearing Ninth Legion examines hard evidence for the
foundation, development, mysterious disappearance, or possi-
ble continuation of Rome's lost Legion.
Paperback: 978-1-84694-559-5 ebook: 978-1-84694-931-9

Readers of ebooks can buy or view any of these bestsellers by clicking on the live link in the title. Most titles are published in paperback and as an ebook. Paperbacks are available in traditional bookshops. Both print and ebook formats are available online.

Find more titles and sign up to our readers' newsletter at
http://www.johnhuntpublishing.com/history-home

Follow us on Facebook at
https://www.facebook.com/ChronosBooks

and Twitter at https://twitter.com/ChronosBooks